Praise for *A Morning and Evening Prayerbook*

"A prayer book for everyone! We've desperately needed this brilliant compilation of authentic, personal prayers from across all ages and expressions of the Church. Profoundly rich in beauty, emotion, and theology, these prayers will nourish and deepen your soul."

—Rick Warren

"If there is such a thing as a 'perfect' prayer book, then [this] is that book. Choosing with an unfailing sensitivity to both beauty and faithful practice, the Gushees have melded the Christian communions and traditions of two thousand years into one rich, melodious, and formative regimen for beginning and ending the Christian day. Their Introduction alone is worth the price of the book."

—Phyllis Tickle, founding editor [ret.],
Publishers Weekly, religion

"This is an astonishing book. It not only orients the reader to devotional prayer in a way that is truly ecumenical, but rather than going for the least common denominator, it somehow manages to stay authentically and broadly connected to major figures and ideas in the tradition. A classic example of finding unity in diversity, it is a book that will serve as an important part of my own family's prayer life for years to come."

—Dr. Charles C. Camosy, assistant professor
of Christian ethics, Fordham University

"A marvelous, diverse collection of prayers mined from the richest of all the major Christian traditions and centuries. A simple yet profound aid for one's personal devotional life."

—Ronald J. Sider, president,
Evangelicals for Social Action

A Morning and Evening

Prayerbook

Jeanie Gushee and
David P. Gushee
Editors

W Publishing Group

An Imprint of Thomas Nelson

Published in Nashville, Tennessee, by W Publishing Group, an imprint of Thomas Nelson.

Thomas Nelson titles may be purchased in bulk for educational, business, fund-raising, or sales promotional use. For information, please e-mail SpecialMarkets@ThomasNelson.com.

Scripture quotations are taken from the New King James Version®. © 1982 by Thomas Nelson, Inc. Used by permission. All rights reserved.

Images that appear in this book are copies of faithful photographic reproductions of original two-dimensional work of art, both woodcut and engraving on copper, that are in the public domain, created by Albrecht Dürer (1471–1528) and found at Wikimedia Commons, commons.wikimedia.org.

Previously published as *Yours Is the Day, Lord, Yours Is the Night*, © 2012 by Thomas Nelson.

ISBN 978-1-4041-0938-4

Library of Congress Cataloging-in-Publication Data

Yours is the day, Lord, yours is the night : a morning and evening prayer book / Jeanie Gushee and David P. Gushee, editors.
    p. cm.
Includes bibliographical references and index.
ISBN 978-0-8499-6448-0 (hardcover)
1. Prayers. 2. Devotional calendars. I. Gushee, Jeanie. II. Gushee, David P., 1962–
BV245.Y68 2012
242'.8—dc23

2012024162

Printed in the United States of America

18 19 20 21 22 LSC 5 4 3 2 1

CONTENTS

INTRODUCTION

This book offers a collection of morning and evening prayers, a different one for every day and night of the year, drawn from the ecumenical treasury of Christian prayer through the ages. We have organized them to reflect the seasons, the holidays, and the liturgical calendar of the Western Christian church. Drawing copiously from Catholic, Protestant, and Eastern Orthodox Christianity, it includes prayers from the Old Testament period and every century from the first century AD to 2012.

A Morning and Evening Prayerbook includes Christian prayers from every continent in the habitable world. It could well be the most ecumenical and comprehensive Christian prayer book to date. As such, we hope it will not only inspire personal Christian devotion but help build a stronger sense of connectedness to Christian tradition and the church universal. (We are reminded of Christ's prayer in John 17:11: "Holy Father, keep through Your name those whom You have given Me, that they may be one as We are.")

As a daily devotional, our prayer book is suitable for use by individuals, couples, families, prayer groups, and churches. We primarily designed it, though, with individuals in mind, to assist Christians in their daily prayer times with God. In some cases the language of the prayers has been altered from collectives ("we," "us") to singulars ("I," "me") in keeping with a primary purpose of serving the devotional lives of individuals.

This book is not meant to serve as a substitute for spontaneous Christian prayers but as a springboard for them. We hope you will use these morning prayers as we do—as a way to wake up and greet the new day with God, inspired by the noble aspirations of some of the heroes of the faith, followed by talking with God about the feelings in our own hearts. Remember that reading a prayer is not the same thing as praying one. These prayers must find an echo in the intentions of your heart to be prayers to God. That may require reading them more than once.

The evening prayers close the day, asking for God's blessing as we lose ourselves in sleep. We find that they combine nicely with a personal prayer as we drift off, thanking God for good aspects of the day just concluded.

The prayers vary in length, but the majority of them are fairly short—and we have abbreviated some for easier use. Some readers may also notice these prayers have not been edited for inclusive language about people and God. Our principle throughout this collection has been to allow these leaders from two thousand years of Christian tradition to speak in their own distinctive voices, so we have chosen not to alter ancient Christian prayers to achieve contemporary gender-neutral norms.

Ancient prayers were written in Greek, Latin, and other languages and sometimes come down through the centuries to us in several different forms. This is why a prayer we cite may be available to you in a different form in other publications.

It is our hope that this book will assist Christians in their daily prayers for a lifetime. The Christian liturgical calendar includes a few holy days that vary from year to year as to the date on which they fall. (Ash Wednesday, for example, begins the Lenten season some years in February, other years in March. Advent, also, arrives sometimes in late November, other years in December.) In whatever year you are praying through this daybook, we suggest that on Ash Wednesday, the days of Holy Week, Easter week, Pentecost, Trinity Sunday, and the first Sunday of Advent, you flip over to the prayers selected for those days. The next day, return to the prayer in the book appropriate for the calendar day.

The apostle Paul instructed followers to "pray without ceasing" (1 Thess. 5:17). It is our prayer for this book that you will use it to honor God and seek Him in prayer each morning and nighttime of the year, each year of your life. Blessings!

—JEANIE AND DAVID GUSHEE

Calendar of Movable Holy Days

	2019	2020	2021	2022	2023
Ash Wednesday	March 6	February 26	February 17	March 2	February 22
Palm Sunday	April 14	April 5	March 28	April 10	April 2
Maundy Thursday	April 18	April 9	April 1	April 14	April 6
Good Friday	April 19	April 10	April 2	April 15	April 7
Easter Sunday	April 21	April 12	April 4	April 17	April 9
Pentecost Sunday	June 9	May 31	May 23	June 5	May 28
Trinity Sunday	June 16	June 7	May 30	June 12	June 4
1st Sunday of Advent	December 1	November 29	November 28	November 27	December 3
2nd Sunday of Advent	December 8	December 6	December 5	December 4	December 10
3rd Sunday of Advent	December 15	December 13	December 12	December 11	December 17
4th Sunday of Advent	December 22	December 20	December 19	December 18	December 24

January 1: New Year's Day

Morning

O sweet Jesus Lord, Thou art the present
portion of Thy people. Favor us with such a
sense this year of Thy preciousness, that from its
first to its last days we may be glad and
rejoice in Thee! Let January open with joy in the Lord
and December close with gladness in Jesus.
Amen.

—Charles Spurgeon (1834–1892)

Evening

Grant, O Lord,
that as the years change,
I may find rest in Your eternal changelessness.
May I meet this new year bravely,
secure in the faith that,
while we come and go,
and life changes around us,
You are always the same,
guiding us with Your wisdom,
and protecting us with Your love.
Amen.

—William Temple (1881–1944)

January 2

Morning

Lord Christ, Alpha and Omega, the beginning and the end,
whose years never fail;
may I so pass through the coming year with a faithful heart,
that in all things I may please You and reflect Your glory;
for You are alive and reign with the Father and the Holy Spirit,
one God, now and for ever.
Amen.

—Mozarabic Sacramentary (7th c.)

Evening

It is well and good, Lord, if all things change,
provided we are rooted in You.
If I go everywhere with You, my God,
everywhere things will happen for Your sake;
that is what I desire.
Amen.

—John of the Cross (1542–1591)

January 3

Morning

Almighty God,
who alone art without variableness or shadow of turning,
and hast safely brought me through the changes of time
to the beginning of another year:
I beseech Thee to pardon the sins that I have
committed in the year which is past;
and give me grace that I may spend
the remainder of my days to Thy honor and glory;
through Jesus Christ our Lord,
Amen.

—Church of Ireland

Evening

I thank You, O God,
for Your care and protection this day,
keeping me from physical harm and spiritual corruption.
I now place the work of the day into Your hands,
trusting that You will redeem my errors,
and turn my achievements to Your glory.
And I now ask You to work within me,
trusting that You will use the hours of rest
to create in me a new heart and new soul. . . .
Let me rest tonight in Your arms,
and so may the dreams that pass through my mind be holy.
And let me awake tomorrow,
strong and eager to serve You.
Amen.

—Jacob Boehme (1575–1624)

January 4

Morning

Lo, fainter now lie spread the shades of night,
And upward spread the trembling gleams of morn;
Suppliant we bend before the Lord of Light,
And pray at early dawn
That His sweet charity may all our sin
Forgive, and make our miseries to cease;
May grant us health, grant us the gift divine
Of everlasting peace.
Father Supreme, this grace on us confer,
And Thou, O Son, by an eternal birth,
With Thee, coequal Spirit comforter,
Whose glory fills the earth!
Amen.

—Gregory the Great (540–604)

Evening

That this evening be holy, good and peaceful:
we pray to You, O Lord.
That Your holy angels may lead us in the paths of peace and goodwill:
we pray to You, O Lord.
That we may be pardoned and forgiven for any sins and offenses:
we pray to You, O Lord. . . .
That we may be bound together by Your Holy Spirit
in communion with all Your saints, entrusting one another
and all our life to Christ:
we pray to You, O Lord.
Amen.

—Eastern Orthodox Litany

January 5

Morning

Faithful Guide,
You sit at the gate of my life,
inviting me to eagerly enter
the newness stretching before me.
As I attend to the old burdens
that have weighed me down with worry,
I look ahead with hopeful expectation
to what my heart most needs. . . .
I seek to let go of what keeps me unloving.
I long to contribute to peace in this world. . . .
Attune me daily to the beauty in all of creation.
Embrace me with Your serenity and tender mercy.
I give You my love as I walk into this new beginning.
Amen.

—Joyce Rupp (1943–)

Evening

Lord, strengthen my soul,
so that so many firm resolutions
may be more than mere words.
Amen.

—Elizabeth Ann Seton (1774–1821)

The Adoration of the Magi

January 6: Epiphany: Manifestation of Christ to the Gentiles

Morning

Beloved Jesus,
may I have the faith and insight of the Wise Men,
who, when faced with an ancient hope of a foreign people
and the appearance of a remarkable star,
grasped the connection, and went and followed that star.
I stand now at the border of a new year,
which is to me like an unknown country.
I don't know what I will experience as I traverse it;
I don't know what obstacles will lie across my path.
Lead me, like the Wise Men, on a quest
of faithfulness and worship,
of hopefulness and giving,
and always unto Yourself.
Amen.

—Jeanie Gushee (1962–)

Evening

O God,
who by the leading of a star didst manifest Thy
only-begotten Son to the peoples of the earth:
lead me, who know Thee now by faith,
to Thy presence,
where I may behold Thy glory face to face;
through Jesus Christ our Lord.
Amen.

—Book of Common Prayer (1979)

January 7

Morning

Strong Son of God, immortal Love,
Whom we, that have not seen Thy face,
By faith, and faith alone, embrace,
Believing where we cannot prove . . .
Thou wilt not leave us in the dust.
Thou madest man, he knows not why;
He thinks he was not made to die;
And Thou hast made him; Thou art just.
Thou seemest human and divine,
The highest, holiest manhood, Thou;
Our wills are ours, we know not how:
Our wills are ours, to make them Thine . . .
We have but faith; we cannot know,
For our knowledge is of things we see;
And yet we trust it comes from Thee,
A beam in darkness: let it grow . . .
Amen.

—Alfred, Lord Tennyson (1809–1892)

Evening

Lord, be with me, and help me by Your Spirit,
to perform all my duties to Your praise.
I pray You be very near to us all;
protect us by Your providential care over us,
and above all, further visit us by Your love, power, and Spirit.
Oh Lord! turn us, and we shall be turned;
help us, and we shall be helped;
keep us, and we shall be kept.
Amen.

—Elizabeth Fry (1780–1845)

January 8

Morning

Almighty and ever-present Father,
Your watchful care reaches from one end of the earth to the other.
You order all things in such power
that even the tensions and tragedies of sin
cannot frustrate Your loving plans.
Help me to embrace Your will,
and give me the strength to follow Your call,
so that Your truth may live in my heart and reflect peace
to those who believe in Your love.
I ask this in the name of Jesus the Lord.
Amen.

—ROMAN SACRAMENTARY (20TH C.)

Evening

Watch, dear Lord,
with those who wake, or watch, or weep tonight,
and give Your angels charge over those who sleep.
Tend Your sick ones, O Lord Christ.
Rest Your weary ones,
bless Your dying ones,
soothe Your suffering ones,
pity Your afflicted ones,
shield Your joyous ones;
and all for Your love's sake.
Amen.

—AUGUSTINE OF HIPPO (354–430)

JANUARY 9

Morning

Deliver me, O God, from a slothful mind,
from all lukewarmness, and all dejection of spirit:
I know these cannot but deaden my love to Thee;
mercifully free my heart from them, and give me
a lively, zealous, active, and cheerful spirit,
that I may vigorously perform whatever Thou commandest,
thankfully suffer whatever Thou choosest for me,
and be ever ardent to obey in all things Thy holy love.
Amen.

—JOHN WESLEY (1703–1791)

Evening

Lord Jesus,
stay with us, for evening is at hand
and the day is past;
be our companion in the way, kindle our hearts,
and awaken hope, that we may know You
as You are revealed in Scripture
and the breaking of bread.
Grant this for the sake of Your love.
Amen.

—BOOK OF COMMON PRAYER (1979)

January 10

Morning

Glory be to Thee, Lord, glory to Thee. . . .
To this day and all days,
a perfect, holy, peaceful, healthy, sinless course,
vouchsafe O Lord.
The Angel of peace, a faithful guide,
guardian of souls and bodies,
to encamp around me,
and ever to prompt what is salutary,
vouchsafe O Lord.
Pardon and remission of all sins and of all offences,
vouchsafe O Lord.
To our souls what is good and convenient,
and peace to the world.
Amen.

—Lancelot Andrewes (1555–1626)

Evening

We give You thanks, O God,
for revealing Your Son Jesus Christ to us
by the light of His resurrection:
grant that as we sing Your glory at the close of this day,
our joy may abound in the morning . . .
through Jesus Christ our Lord.
Amen.

—Book of Common Prayer (1979)

January 11

Morning

My God,
I love You with my whole heart and soul, and above all things,
because You are infinitely good and perfect,
and most worthy of all my love;
and for Your sake I love my neighbor as myself.
Mercifully grant, O my God,
that having loved You on earth,
I may love and enjoy You forever in heaven.
Amen.

—Traditional Catholic prayer

Evening

Most High, Glorious God,
enlighten the darkness of our minds.
Give us a right faith, a firm hope, and a perfect charity,
so that we may always and in all things act
according to Your Holy Will.
Amen.

—Francis of Assisi (1181–1226)

January 12

Morning

All this day, O Lord,
let me touch as many lives as possible for Thee;
and every life I touch, do Thou by Thy Spirit quicken,
whether through the word I speak,
the prayer I breathe, or the life I live.
Amen.

—Mary Sumner (1828–1921)

Evening

Lord,
Abide with me,
Fast falls the eventide;
The darkness deepens,
Lord, with me abide;
When other helpers fail
And comforts flee,
Help of the helpless,
O abide with me.
Amen.

—Henry Francis Lyte (1793–1847)

January 13

Morning

Make me to remember, O God, that every
day is Thy gift, and ought to be used
according to Thy command;
through Jesus Christ our Lord.
Amen.

—Samuel Johnson (1709–1784)

Evening

Jesus Christ,
the Love that gives love,
You are higher than the highest star;
You are deeper than the deepest sea;
You cherish us as Your own family;
You embrace us as Your own spouse;
You rule over us as Your own subjects;
You welcome us as Your dearest friend.
Let all the world worship You.
Amen.

—Hildegard of Bingen (1098–1179)

January 14

Morning

Lord, help me to use honestly and well this day
all the talents which You have given me,
that the gain may not be mine only, but Yours
and Your kingdom's;
through Jesus Christ our Lord.
Amen.

—COMMON WORSHIP: DAILY PRAYER (2005)

Evening

Look down, O Lord,
from Your heavenly throne,
illumine the darkness of this night with Your celestial brightness,
and from the children of light,
banish the deeds of darkness;
through Jesus Christ our Lord.
Amen.

—AMBROSIAN SACRAMENTARY (5TH C.)

January 15

Morning

O God,
who hast folded back the mantle of the night to
clothe us in the golden glory of the day, chase
from my heart all gloomy thoughts, and make me
glad with the brightness of hope,
that I may effectively aspire to unwon virtues,
through Jesus Christ our Lord.
Amen.

—Gregorian Sacramentary (8th c.)

Evening

Lord God,
send peaceful sleep to renew our tired bodies.
May Your help always renew us and keep us strong in Your service.
Into Your hands, O Lord, we commend our souls and bodies,
beseeching You to keep us this night under Your protection,
and strengthen us for our service on the morrow, for Christ's sake.
Amen.

—Archbishop William Laud (1573–1645)

JANUARY 16

Morning

O God,
I ask today that You
prepare my spirit for this day's temptations,
which may come in forms not easily recognized.
The temptation to pride—to envy—to anger;
the temptation to doubt—to cynicism—to hopelessness;
the temptation to a faith merely of words and not of deeds.
May my every free choice today
express my lifetime decision
to submit my will to Yours.
For You are not just "Lord"—
You are my Lord.
I am Yours.
Amen.

—David P. Gushee (1962–)

Evening

As my head rests on my pillow,
let my soul rest in Your mercy.
As my limbs relax on my mattress,
let my soul relax in Your peace.
As my body finds warmth beneath blankets,
let my soul find warmth in Your love.
As my mind is filled with dreams,
let my soul be filled with visions of Your Heaven.
Amen.

—Johann Freylinghausen (1670–1739)

January 17

Morning

O God, through the grace of Your Holy Spirit,
You pour Your best gift of love
into the hearts of Your faithful people.
Grant unto me health, both of mind and body,
that I may love You with my whole strength,
and that today I may do those things
which please You, to Your entire satisfaction;
through Christ our Lord.
Amen.

—Sarum Rite Liturgy (11th c.)

Evening

O Lord, support us all the day long of this troublous life
until the shadows lengthen,
and the evening comes,
the busy world is hushed,
the fever of life is over, and our work is done.
Then Lord, in Thy mercy, grant us a safe lodging,
and a holy rest, and peace at the last.
Amen.

—Cardinal John Henry Newman (1801–1890)

January 18

Into Thy hands, O Lord, I commend myself
this day. Let Thy presence be with me to
its close. Strengthen me to remember that in
whatsoever good work I do I am serving Thee.
Give me a diligent and watchful spirit,
that I may seek in all things to know Thy will,
and knowing it, gladly to perform it, to the
honor of Thy name.
Amen.

—GELASIAN SACRAMENTARY (8TH C.)

Evening

Almighty God,
from whom all thoughts of truth and peace proceed,
kindle, I pray You, in the hearts of all people
the true love of peace . . .
that in tranquility Your kingdom may go forward,
till the whole earth is filled
with the knowledge of Your love;
through Jesus Christ our Lord.
Amen.

—BOOK OF COMMON PRAYER (1928)

JANUARY 19

Morning

I give Thee hearty thanks, O God, for the rest of
the past night and for the gift of a new day
with its opportunities of pleasing Thee.
Grant that I so pass its hours in the
perfect freedom of Thy service, that at eventide
I may again give thanks unto Thee;
through Jesus Christ our Lord.
Amen.

—DAYBREAK OFFICE OF THE EASTERN CHURCH (6TH C.)

Evening

Set free, O Lord, the souls of Your servants
from all restlessness and anxiety.
Give us that peace and power which flow from You.
Keep us in all perplexity and distress,
that upheld by Your strength and stayed on the rock of Your faithfulness,
we may abide in You now and evermore.
Amen.

—FRANCIS PAGET (1851–1911)

January 20

Morning

Thou alone knowest best what is for my good.
As I am not my own but altogether Thine,
so neither do I desire that my will be done,
but Thine,
nor will I have any will but Thine.
Amen.

—Francis Borgia (1510–1572)

Evening

God, You are peace everlasting,
whose chosen reward is the gift of peace,
and You have taught us that the peacemakers are Your children.
Pour Your grace into our souls,
that everything discordant may utterly vanish,
and all that makes for peace be sweet to us for ever;
through Jesus Christ our Lord.
Amen.

—Charles Kingsley (1819–1875)

January 21

Morning

Blessed art Thou, O Lord our God. . . .
Grant that I may become a child of the light,
and of the day. . . . Preserve this day from any
evil of mine, and me from the evils of this day.
Let this day add some knowledge, or good deed,
to yesterday . . .
Amen.

—Lancelot Andrewes (1555–1626)

Evening

Spirit of God, with Your holy breath
You cleanse the hearts and minds of Your people;
You comfort them when they are in sorrow;
You lead them when they wander from the way;
You kindle them when they are cold;
You knot them together when they are at variance;
and You enrich them with many and various gifts.
We beseech You daily to increase
those gifts which You have entrusted to us;
that with Your light before us and within us
we may pass through this world
without stumbling and without straying.
Amen.

—Erasmus (1466–1536)

Morning

O Thou good Omnipotent,
who so carest for every one of us, as if Thou caredst for him alone . . .
blessed is the man who loveth Thee,
and his friend in Thee, and his enemy for Thee;
for he only loses none dear to him,
to whom all are dear in Him who cannot be lost.
And who is that but our God,
that made heaven and earth, and filleth them . . .
And Thy law is truth, and truth is Thyself.
I behold how some things pass away that others may replace them,
but Thou dost never depart, O God, my Father supremely good,
Beauty of all beautiful.
To Thee will I entrust whatsoever I have received from Thee,
so shall I lose nothing.
Thou madest me for Thyself
and my heart is restless until it repose in Thee.
Amen.

—Augustine of Hippo (354–430)

Evening

Save us, O Lord, while waking, and guard us while sleeping,
that when we wake, we may watch with Christ,
and when we sleep, we may rest in peace.
Amen.

—Compline prayer in Roman Catholic Breviary

Morning

O Lord our God, as Thou hast in mercy
preserved me to the beginning of another day,
enable me by Thy grace to live to Thee,
and to set my affections on things above,
not on things upon the earth.
Pour into my mind the light of Thy truth,
and cause me to rejoice in Thy word.
Shed abroad Thy love in my heart,
and bestow upon me abundantly the peace and
comfort of Thy Holy Spirit;
for the sake of Jesus Christ our Lord.
Amen.

—Isaac Ashe (d. 1888)

Evening

Abide with us, Lord,
for it is toward evening
and the day is far spent.
Abide with us and with Your whole Church.
Abide with us in the evening of the day, in the evening of our life,
and in the evening of the world.
Abide with us and with all Your faithful ones,
O Lord, in time and eternity.
Amen.

—Lutheran Manual of Prayer

January 24

Morning

Let me do Your will today, good Father.
That is what I really want.
I admit that I cannot direct my life as well as You can.
Often I get confused, or focused on myself.
But You, whose power made the intricate world,
can direct my minutes and my hours today.
Help me remember to walk with You, and not ahead,
to consult You in the decisions of my day.
I believe that Your way for me is always right.
Help me to honor You, to be happy,
and to bless the world today.
Amen.

—Jeanie Gushee (1962–)

Evening

Great, O Lord, is Your kingdom, Your power, and Your glory;
great also is Your wisdom, Your goodness, Your justice, Your mercy;
and for all these we bless You,
and will magnify Your name for ever and ever.
Amen.

—George Wither (1588–1667)

Morning

May Your Spirit guide my mind,
which is so often dull and empty.
Let my thoughts always be on You,
and let me see You in all things.
May Your Spirit quicken my soul,
which is so often listless and lethargic.
Let my soul be awake to Your presence,
and let me know You in all things.
Amen.

—Johann Freylinghausen (1670–1739)

Evening

My God, I love You above all else, and I desire to end my life with You.
Always and in all things with my whole heart and strength I seek You.
If You do not give Yourself to me, You give me nothing;
if I do not find You, I find nothing.
Grant, therefore, most gracious God,
that I may always love You for Your own sake more than anything else,
and seek You always and everywhere in this present life,
so that at the last I may find You
and for ever hold fast to You in the life to come.
Grant this for the sake of Jesus Christ our Lord.
Amen.

—Thomas Bradwardine (c. 1290–1349)

January 26

Morning

Lord, since You exist, we exist.
Since You are beautiful, we are beautiful.
Since You are good, we are good.
By our existence we honor You.
By our beauty we glorify You.
By our goodness we love You.
Lord, through Your power all things were made.
Through Your wisdom all things are governed.
Through Your grace all things are sustained.
Give us power to serve You,
wisdom to discern Your laws,
and grace to obey them at all times.
Amen.

—Edmund of Abingdon (c. 1180–1240)

Evening

You are holy, Lord, the only God,
and Your deeds are wonderful . . .
You are Good, all Good,
supreme Good,
Lord God, living and true.
You are love.
You are wisdom.
You are humility.
You are endurance.
You are rest.
You are peace.
You are joy and gladness.
You are justice and moderation.
You are all our riches,
and You suffice for us . . .
Amen.

—Francis of Assisi (1181–1226)

Morning

Lord, in union with Your love,
unite my work with Your great work, and perfect it.
As a drop of water poured into a river
is taken up into the activities of the river,
so may my labor become part of Your work.
Thus may those among whom I live and work
be drawn into Your love.
Amen.

—GERTRUDE THE GREAT (1256–c. 1302)

Evening

O Thou whose pow'r o'er moving worlds presides,
Whose voice created, and whose wisdom guides. . . .
'Tis Thine alone to calm the pious breast
With silent confidence and holy rest:
From Thee, great God, we spring, to Thee we tend,
Path, motive, guide, original, and end.
Amen.

—BOETHIUS (c. 480–524); TRANSLATED BY SAMUEL JOHNSON
(1709–1784)

January 28

Morning

Almighty God in Trinity
From all my heart be thanks to Thee
For Thy good deed, that Thou me wrought,
And with Thy precious blood me bought,
And for all good Thou lendst to me,
O Lord God, blessed may Thou be!
All honour, joy and all loving
Be to Thy name without ending.
Amen.

—Richard Rolle (1295–1349)

Evening

Blessed are Thou, O Lord, God of our fathers,
that didst create changes of days and nights,
that hast delivered us from the evil of this day,
that has bestowed on us occasions of joy in the evening
to get us through the night fearlessly in hope:
for Thou art our light, salvation and strength of life—
of whom then shall we be afraid?
Glory be to Thee, O Lord, glory be to Thee,
for all Thy divine perfections,
for Thine inexpressible and unimaginable goodness and mercy. . . .
Glory and praise and blessing and thanksgiving
by the voices and concert of voices
as well of angels as of men,
and of all Thy saints in heaven,
and of all Thy creation withal on earth.
Amen.

—Lancelot Andrewes (1555–1626)

Morning

O King of glory and Lord of valors . . .
who hast said "Be of good cheer; I have overcome the
world": be victorious in me Your servant.
Grant Your compassion to go before me,
Your compassion to come behind me:
before me in my undertakings,
behind me in my ending.
And what will I now say,
unless that Your will be done,
who wills that all should be saved?
Your will is my salvation, my glory,
my joy.
Amen.

—Alcuin of York (c. 735–804)

Evening

O God,
with whom there is no darkness,
but the night shines as the day:
keep and defend us and all Your children,
we beseech You,
throughout the coming night.
Renew our hearts with Your forgiveness,
and our bodies with untroubled sleep,
that we may wake to use more faithfully Your gift of life,
through Jesus Christ, our Lord.
Amen.

—Traditional Catholic prayer

January 30

Morning

Lord God Almighty, Shaper and Ruler of all creatures,
I pray Thee for Thy great mercy,
that Thou guide me, better than I have done, towards Thee.
And guide me to Thy will to the need of my soul, better than I can myself.
And steadfast my mind towards Thy will and to my soul's need.
And strengthen me against the temptations of the devil,
and put far from me all lust, and every unrighteousness,
and shield me against my foes, seen and unseen.
And teach me to do Thy will,
that I may inwardly love Thee before all things, with a pure mind.
For Thou art my Maker and my Redeemer,
my Help, my Comfort, my Trust, my Hope;
praise and glory be to Thee now, ever and ever, world without end.
Amen.

—King Alfred the Great of Wessex (849–899)

Evening

O Lord,
calm the waves of this heart, calm its tempests!
Calm yourself, O my soul,
so that the divine can act in you!
Calm yourself, O my soul,
so that God is able to repose in you, so that His peace may cover you!
Yes, Father in heaven, often have I found
that the world cannot give me peace,
but make me feel that You are able to give me peace;
let me know the truth of Your promise:
that the world may not be able to take away Your peace.
Amen.

—Søren Kierkegaard (1813–1855)

Morning

O Lord God, in whom I live and move and have my being,
open my eyes that I may behold Thy fatherly presence ever about me.
Draw my heart to Thee with the power of Thy love.
Teach me to be anxious for nothing,
and when I have done what Thou hast given me to do,
help me, O God my Savior, to leave the issue to Thy wisdom.
Take from me all doubt and mistrust.
Lift my thoughts up to Thee,
and make me to know that all things are possible to me
through Thy Son my Redeemer.
Amen.

—Brooke Foss Westcott (1825–1901)

Evening

Great and most high God,
You alone possess immortality and dwell in unapproachable light.
You made all creation with wisdom, dividing light from darkness,
establishing the sun to rule the day
and the moon and stars to rule the night.
You have allowed me, a sinner,
to approach Your presence with thanksgiving in this present hour
and to offer You every praise.
O Lord, Lover of us all,
make my prayer ascend to You like incense,
and accept it as a sweet fragrance.
Grant that I may spend the present evening
and the coming night in peace;
clothe me with the armor of light.
Deliver me from the fears of the night
and from everything that lurks about in darkness.
Amen.

—Vespers Liturgy, Eastern Rite Catholic Church

FEBRUARY 1

Morning

Grant me, I beseech Thee, my God,
in the name of Jesus Christ Thy Son,
the charity which never fails,
that my light may shine,
warming my own heart
and enlightening others.
Amen.

COLUMBANUS (c. 550–615)

Evening

Glory to Thee, my God this night
For all the blessings of the light;
Keep me, O keep me, King of Kings,
Beneath Thine own almighty wings.
Forgive me, Lord, for Thy dear Son,
The ill that I this day have done,
That with the world, myself, and Thee
I, ere I sleep, at peace may be.
Teach me to live, that I may dread
The grave as little as my bed;
Teach me to die, that so I may
Triumphing rise at the last day. . . .
Praise God, from whom all blessings flow;
Praise Him, all creatures here below;
Praise Him above, ye heavenly host;
Praise Father, Son, and Holy Ghost.
Amen.

—BISHOP THOMAS KEN (1637–1711)

THE PRESENTATION OF CHRIST IN THE TEMPLE

February 2: Candlemas/Feast of the Presentation of Jesus in the Temple

Morning

Lord Jesus Christ,
You are the true Light enlightening every soul born into this world.
Today we celebrate the feast of Candlemas. . . .
Help us to realize, this day and every day,
that our own humdrum daily work, if it is done for love of You . . .
will be a supernatural work, and will shine brightly
before You for all eternity. . . .
Help us to live in the Light, to make it our own,
and to kindle it in the souls of others,
increasing the area of light and lessening the darkness of the world.
This, dear Lord, help us do. . . .
Then we, too, working for You,
shall be light-bearers who will help to spread Your kingdom on earth,
and increase the number of those who dwell in heaven,
the city of eternal light.
Amen.

—Anonymous Catholic prayer

Evening

Lord, now lettest Thou Thy servant depart in peace,
according to Thy word;
for mine eyes have seen Thy salvation,
which Thou hast prepared
before the face of all people;
a light to lighten the Gentiles,
and the glory of Thy people Israel.
Glory to the Father, and to the Son, and to the Holy Spirit:
as it was in the beginning, is now, and will be forever.
Amen.

—*Nunc Dimittis*, based on Luke 2:29–32

Morning

O God,
I begin this day by remembering who You are:
a righteous God
who responds to our rebellion
not with condemnation but infinite love,
in Jesus Christ Your Son.
May I remember who You are today,
and therefore who I am,
and how I am to live.
Amen.

—DAVID P. GUSHEE (1962–)

Evening

Thou, O Lord,
hast made us glad by Thy works;
in the works of Thy hands shall we rejoice.
Lift up the Light of Thy countenance upon us, O Lord!
Thou hast put joy in my heart.
With the fruit of wheat, wine, and oil have I been satisfied.
In peace I will lie down and sleep,
for Thou alone, O Lord,
makest me to dwell in hope.
Amen.

—EASTERN ORTHODOX PRAYER

FEBRUARY 4

Morning

O Lord, this is my desire,
to walk along the path of life that You have appointed me,
in steadfastness of faith,
in lowliness of heart,
in gentleness of love.
Let not the cares or duties of this life press on me too heavily;
but lighten my burdens,
that I may follow Your way in quietness,
filled with thankfulness for Your mercy, . . .
through Jesus Christ our Lord.
Amen.

—MARIA HARE (1798–1870)

Evening

O God of peace,
who hast taught us that in returning and rest
we shall be saved,
in quietness and in confidence
shall be our strength:
by the might of Thy Spirit
lift me, I pray Thee,
to Thy presence,
where I may be still
and know that Thou art God.
Amen.

—BOOK OF COMMON PRAYER (1979)

Morning

Let the eternal God be the portion of my soul;
let heaven be my inheritance and hope;
let Christ be my Head, and my promise of security;
let faith be my wisdom,
and love my very heart and will,
and patient persevering obedience be my life;
and then I can spare the wisdom of the world,
because I can spare the trifles that it seeks,
and all that they are like to get by it.
Amen.

—RICHARD BAXTER (1615–1691)

Evening

Lord, I see clearly that any affection which I have ever had
is scarcely as one drop in the vast ocean of all the seas,
when compared with the tenderness of Your divine Heart
towards those whom I love. . . .
Therefore I cannot even by one thought wish anything
other than that which Your almighty wisdom
has appointed for each of them. . . .
Lord, bless Your special friends and mine,
according to the good pleasure of Your divine goodness.
Amen.

—GERTRUDE THE GREAT (1256–c. 1302)

FEBRUARY 6

Morning

O God, by whom the world is governed and preserved,
I, Thine unworthy servant, draw nigh unto Thee
to offer my morning sacrifice of prayer and praise.
May I remember that every day is Thy gift,
to be used in Thy service.
Enable me to resist all evil, and dispose me
to follow the guidance of Thy good Spirit,
not trusting to my own strength or wisdom,
but looking to Thee to establish me in every
good word and work;
through Jesus Christ our Lord.
Amen.

—CHARLES JAMES BLOMFIELD (1786–1857)

Evening

O Lord Jesus Christ,
our watchman and keeper,
take us into Thy care,
and grant that, our bodies sleeping,
our minds may watch in Thee
and be made merry by some sight of that celestial and heavenly life
wherein Thou art the King and Prince,
together with the Father and the Holy Ghost,
where the angels and holy souls be most happy citizens.
O purify our souls, keep clean our bodies,
that in both we may please Thee,
sleeping and waking, for ever.
Amen.

—CHRISTIAN PRAYER (1566)

FEBRUARY 7

Morning

Almighty God, unto whom all hearts are open,
all desires known, and from whom no secrets are hid:
cleanse the thoughts of our hearts by the inspiration of Thy Holy Spirit,
that we may perfectly love Thee, and worthily magnify Thy holy Name;
through Christ our Lord.
Amen.

—BOOK OF COMMON PRAYER (1979)

Evening

O Merciful God, eternal light, shining in darkness . . .
since Thou hast appointed the night for rest and the day for labor,
we beseech Thee grant that our bodies may rest in peace and quietness,
that afterward they may be able to endure the labor they must bear. . . .
Defend us against all assaults of the devil and take us
into Thy holy protection.
And although we have not passed this day
without greatly sinning against Thee,
we beseech Thee to hide our sins with Thy mercy,
as Thou hidest all things on Earth with the darkness of the night . . .
through Jesus Christ our Lord.
Amen.

—JOHN CALVIN (1509–1564)

FEBRUARY 8

Morning

Stay with me, and then I shall begin to shine as Thou shinest:
so to shine as to be a light to others.
The light, O Jesus, will be all from Thee.
None of it will be mine. No merit to me.
It will be Thou who shinest through me upon others.
O let me thus praise Thee,
in the way which Thou dost love best,
by shining on all those around me.
Give light to them as well as to me;
light them with me, through me.
Amen.

— CARDINAL JOHN HENRY NEWMAN (1801–1890)

Evening

The day is Yours, the night also is Yours;
You have prepared the light and the sun.
You have set all the borders of the earth;
You have made summer and winter.
Remember this, that the enemy has reproached, O LORD,
And that a foolish people has blasphemed Your name.
Oh, do not deliver the life of Your turtledove to the wild beast!
Do not forget the life of Your poor forever.
Amen.

— PSALM 74:16–19

Morning

Having arisen from sleep, I fall down before Thee, O blessed One,
and sing to Thee, O mighty One, the angelic hymn:
Holy, holy, holy art Thou, O God!
Amen.

—EASTERN ORTHODOX PRAYER

Evening

Grant us, O Lord, the blessing of those whose minds are stayed on You,
so that we may be kept in perfect peace: a peace which cannot be broken.
Let not our minds rest upon any creature, but only in the Creator;
not upon goods, things, houses, lands,
inventions of vanities, or foolish fashions,
lest, our peace being broken, we become cross and brittle
and given over to envy.
From all such deliver us, O God, and grant us Your peace.
Amen.

—GEORGE FOX (1624–1691)

FEBRUARY 10

Morning

O Thou most holy and ever loving God,
I thank Thee once more for the quiet rest
of the night that has gone by,
for the new promise that has come with this
fresh morning, and for the hope of this day . . .
Amen.

—ROBERT COLLYER (1823–1912)

Evening

O Lord God Almighty,
as You have taught us to call the evening,
the morning, and the noonday one day;
and have made the sun to know its going down:
dispel the darkness of our hearts,
that by Your brightness we may know You to be
the true God and eternal light,
living and reigning for ever and ever.
Amen.

—BOOK OF COMMON PRAYER (1979)

FEBRUARY 11

Morning

God of light, eternal and bright-shining,
do not allow the noises and shadows of this fleeting world to confuse us.
Do not allow the deceptions of the world to muddle us.
Give us strength to bear and face willingly the evils that we encounter;
and do not allow Your provident goodness to puff us up.
The faith that You promised us, God,
please faithfully render it, and we will repay You.
Amen.

—CLARE OF ASSISI (1194–1253)

Evening

O God, who are peace everlasting,
whose chosen reward is the gift of peace,
and who has taught us that the peacemakers are Your children:
pour Your peace into our hearts,
that everything discordant may utterly vanish,
and that all that makes for peace be loved and sought by us always;
through Jesus Christ our Lord.
Amen.

—MOZARABIC SACRAMENTARY (7TH C.)

FEBRUARY 12

Morning

Let Your mighty outstretched arm, O Lord, be my defense;
Your mercy and loving-kindness in Jesus Christ,
Your dear Son, my salvation;
Your true word my instruction;
the grace of Your life-giving Spirit my comfort and consolation,
to the end and in the end;
through the same Jesus Christ our Lord.
Amen.

—JOHN KNOX (1505–1572)

Evening

Abide with us, Lord, for it is toward evening
and the day is far spent.
Yea, the shadows of the evening are stretched out
and the day is declining upon us.
Turn Thee again, O Lord, at the last
and be gracious unto Thy servants.
Let Your merciful kindness, O Lord, be upon us,
as we do put our trust in Thee . . .
Amen.

—*THE BOOK OF HOURS* (1866)

LENT

Each year Ash Wednesday begins the church season of Lent, the six-week period that ends at Easter. Ash Wednesday contains all the emphases of Lent. At church ashes are placed on our foreheads in the sign of the cross, serving a threefold gospel purpose.

First, these ashes remind us that the destiny of our earthly bodies is "ashes to ashes, dust to dust," so we must develop our souls, which will not die.

Second, wearing the sign of the cross on our foreheads shows those who see us on Ash Wednesday that we are followers of Christ and His Way. This is a wordless testimony to a godless world. It also often leads to conversations wherein we can give "a reason for the hope that is in [us]" (1 Peter 3:15).

Third, wearing ashes has been a sign of remorse since Old Testament times. And penitence is primarily what Lent is about. It is true we have a great hope of life with God when we die and of a new heaven and a new earth that God will unveil at the end of time. But in the meantime this world is surfeited with sin, with plentiful injustice and hurt. We are right to feel serious, to feel sad when we consider the wounds of the world and especially how our own sins and selfishness contribute to them. Jesus died for the love of sinners, and we need to reflect on how our sins helped to slay Him.

So for six weeks each year during Lent, we reflect on our lives and seek to uproot the sin there. We recollect the transience of our mortal life. Sometimes we abstain from foods and luxuries, and these abstentions may be noticed by others and give us opportunities to share our faith. We give our money and help to the needy, and this in turn helps us tamp down our sins of avarice and indifference.

Above all we honor Christ in prayer for His friendship and His sacrifice for us.

February 13: Ash Wednesday

Morning

Gracious and loving God,
the seasons of Christmas and Epiphany have passed,
and here a new Lent has begun.
I thank You for Your active presence in my busy life;
for the opportunities given, and the blessings received.
As I embrace this new season of reflection,
breathe freely through me and renew my spirit with fresh resolve and purpose.
Give me grace to be a good steward of all that You have entrusted to me.
Give me grace to serve You with a generous,
compassionate, and loving heart.
Bless these Lenten days ahead. Give me the courage to be faithful,
and show me how to proclaim the Good News of Your Son.
Amen.

—Anonymous

Evening

You, Lord, brought into being the everlasting fabric of the universe;
You wove the tapestry of life.
From one generation to another You are constant and righteous in Your laws,
wise and prudent in Your actions.
To look round is to see Your goodness;
to trust You is to know Your generosity;
to confess to You is to receive Your forgiveness.
Make us clean with the strong soap of Your truth.
Make us whole with the powerful medicine of Your grace.
Show us the light of Your smile. Protect us with Your mighty arm.
Save us from all wrong-doing by Your outstretched arm. . . .
To You, who alone can grant to us those and all good things,
we offer up our praise through Jesus Christ,
the high priest and guardian of our souls.
Amen.

—Clement of Rome (d. 100)

February 14: Lent; Valentine's Day

Morning

O God, who by love alone are great and glorious,
who are present and live with me by love alone:
grant me likewise by love to attain another self,
by love to live in others,
and by love to come to my glory to see and
accompany Your love throughout all eternity.
Amen.

—Thomas Traherne (1636–1674)

Evening

Good night! Good night!
Far flies the light;
But still God's love
Shall flame above,
Making all bright.
Good night! Good night!
Amen.

—Victor Hugo (1802–1885)

February 15: Lent

Morning

Give me, O Lord,
patience and sense of purpose in each
of the things which You send to beset me . . .
Please protect me through the dangers and confusion
of my transient life on earth,
ensuring that in all things I strive for eternal
life in Heaven. I know that I am very
slow to make amends for my sins,
despite the many favors You grant me.
Fix my trust, my timid hopes, upon Yourself,
so that I may stand on a secure foundation.
Lift up my thoughts with Your wisdom . . .
Amen.

—The Exeter Book (c. 950)

Evening

O Lord, keep Thyself present to us ever,
and perfect Thy strength in our weakness.
Take us and ours under Thy blessed care,
this night and evermore; through Jesus Christ our Lord.
Amen.

—Thomas Arnold (1795–1842)

February 16: Lent

Morning

O Thou who in almighty power wast meek,
and in perfect excellence was lowly,
grant unto us the same mind,
that we may mourn over our evil will.
Our bodies are frail and fading;
our minds are blind and forward;
all that we have which is our own is naught;
if we have any good in us it is wholly Thy gift.
O Savior, since Thou, the Lord of heaven and earth,
didst humble Thyself, grant unto us true humility,
and make us like Thyself; and then, of infinite goodness,
raise us to Thine everlasting glory;
who livest and reignest with the Father and the Holy Ghost,
for ever and for ever.
Amen.

—Thomas Cranmer (1489–1556)

Evening

Lord Jesus,
bind me to You and to my neighbor with love.
May my heart not be turned away from You.
May my soul not be deceived
nor my talent or mind enticed by allurements of error,
so that I may never distance myself from Your love.
Thus may I love my neighbor as myself,
with strength, wisdom, and gentleness,
with Your help, You who are blessed throughout all ages.
Amen.

—Anthony of Padua (1195–1231)

February 17: Lent

Morning

We beseech You, O Lord,
that as our bodies grow weaker for lack of food
during the season of fasting,
so our souls may grow stronger.
May we learn to fight more valiantly
against evil,
and strive more earnestly for righteousness.
Thus, through abstaining from the fruits of the earth,
may we bear more abundantly the
fruits of Your Spirit.
Amen.

—Gelasian Sacramentary (8th c.)

Evening

O my God, I give myself to You as my origin;
possess me wholly.
May I ever remain in You;
may I avoid all that may not be worthy of my origin.
May You be the beginning and end of all my actions. . . .
O my God, I give myself to You as my prototype.
Imprint upon my soul a perfect likeness of Yourself.
I give myself to You as my ruler and my protector.
Direct me according to Your holy will and preserve me from sin.
I give and abandon myself to You as my sovereign.
Do with me what You will.
I give myself to You as my judge.
Willingly I submit to all the judgments You have exercised
and ever will exercise upon me, in time and in eternity.
Amen.

—John Eudes (1601–1680)

February 18: Lent

O Jesus,
keep me under the standard of Your cross.
Let me not just look at You crucified,
but have You living in my heart.
Amen.

—Bernadette of Lourdes (1844–1879)

Evening

O eternal Mercy, You who cover over Your creatures' faults!
It does not surprise me that You say of those
who leave deadly sin behind and return to You:
"I will not remember that you had ever offended me."
O unspeakable mercy!
I am not surprised that You speak so to those who forsake sin,
when You say of those who persecute you:
"I want You to pray to me for them so that I can be merciful to them."
What mercy comes forth from Your Godhead, eternal Father,
to rule the whole world with Your power! . . .
Your mercy is life-giving. It is the light in which both the upright
and sinners discover Your goodness.
Your mercy shines forth in Your saints in the height of heaven.
And if I turn to the earth, Your mercy is everywhere. . . .
In mercy You cleansed us in the blood;
in mercy You kept company with Your creatures.
O mad Lover! It was not enough for You to take on our humanity:
You had to die as well!
O mercy! My heart is engulfed with the thought of You!
For wherever I turn my thoughts I find nothing but mercy!
O eternal Father, forgive my foolish presumption
in babbling on so before You—
but Your merciful love is my excuse in the presence of Your kindness.
Amen.

—Catherine of Siena (1347–1380)

FEBRUARY 19: LENT

Morning

Let me hold fast to You, beautiful Lord,
whom the angels themselves yearn to look upon.
Wherever You go, I will follow You. . . .
You carry my griefs, because You grieve for my sake.
You passed through the narrow doorway
from death to life,
to make it wide enough for all to follow.
Nothing can ever now separate me from Your love.
Amen.

—BERNARD OF CLAIRVAUX (1090–1153)

Evening

O Lord,
forgive what I have been.
Sanctify what I am.
And order what I shall be.
Amen.

—ANONYMOUS

Morning

Lord Jesus Christ,
You stretched out Your arms of love
on the hard wood of the cross
that everyone might come within
the reach of Your saving embrace.
So clothe us in Your Spirit
that we, reaching forth our hands in love,
may bring those who do not know You
to the knowledge and love of You;
for the honor of Your Name.
Amen.

—CHARLES HENRY BRENT (1862–1929)

Evening

Keep me, O Lord,
while I tarry on this earth,
in a serious seeking after Thee,
and in an affectionate walking with Thee,
every day of my life;
that when Thou comest, I may be found not hiding my talent,
nor serving the flesh,
nor yet asleep with my lamp unfurnished,
but waiting and longing for our Lord,
our glorious King,
forever and ever.
Amen.

—RICHARD BAXTER (1615–1691)

Morning

God Almighty, eternal, righteous, and merciful,
give to us poor sinners to do for Your sake
all that we know of Your will,
and to will always what pleases You,
so that, inwardly purified, enlightened,
and kindled by the fire of the Holy Spirit,
we may follow in the footsteps
of Your well-beloved Son, our Lord Jesus Christ.
Amen.

—Francis of Assisi (1181–1226)

Evening

My God,
I pray that I may so know You and love you,
that I may rejoice in You.
And if I may not do so fully in this life,
let me go steadily on to the day when I come to that in fullness.
Let the knowledge of You increase in me here.
Let Your love grow in me here,
and there let it be fulfilled,
so that here my joy may be in a great hope,
and there in full reality.
Amen.

—Anselm of Canterbury (1033–1109)

Morning

Lord,
for our sake You fought and overcame
the temptations in the wilderness.
I pray that I may have the strength
to fight against our enemy the devil.
Be with me today in my thoughts and plans . . .
through Jesus Christ our Lord.
Amen.

—ANGLICAN CHURCH OF PAPUA NEW GUINEA

Evening

O Searcher of hearts, Thou knowest us better than we know ourselves,
and seest the sins which our sinfulness hides from us.
Yet even our own conscience beareth witness against us,
that we often slumber on our appointed watch;
that we talk not always lovingly with each other, and humbly with Thee;
and we withhold that entire sacrifice of ourselves to Thy perfect will. . . .
Oh, look upon our contrition, and lift up our weakness,
and let the dayspring yet arise within our hearts,
and bring us healing, strength, and joy.
Day by day may we grow in faith, in self-denial,
in charity, in heavenly-mindedness.
And then, mingle us at last with the mighty host of Thy redeemed
for evermore.
Amen.

—JAMES MARTINEAU (1805–1900)

Morning

O Heavenly King,
Comforter, Spirit of truth,
everywhere present
and filling all things,
Treasury of blessings
and Giver of life:
come and abide in us.
Cleanse us from every impurity,
and save our souls,
O Good One.
Amen.

—Eastern Orthodox Liturgy

Evening

Almighty and everlasting God,
You hate nothing that You have made,
and do forgive the sins of all those who are penitent;
create and make in us new and contrite hearts, that we,
worthily lamenting our sins and acknowledging our wretchedness,
may obtain of You,
the God of all mercy,
perfect remission and forgiveness;
through Jesus Christ our Lord.
Amen.

—Book of Common Prayer (1928)

Morning

Lord, I make You a present of myself.
I do not know what to do with myself.
Let me, then, Lord, make this exchange:
I will place this evil being into Your hands.
You are the only one who can hide it in Your goodness
and can so rule over me
that nothing will be seen of my own proper self.
On Your part, You will grant Your pure love . . .
Amen.

—CATHERINE OF GENOA (1447–1510)

Evening

Lord Jesus,
You are my light in the darkness;
You are my warmth in the cold;
You are my happiness in sorrow.
Amen.

—ANONYMOUS

February 25: Lent

Morning

Joy, with peace,
amendment of life,
time for true repentance,
the grace and comfort of the Holy Spirit
and perseverance in good works,
grant us, O almighty and merciful Lord.
Amen.

—*Enriching the Christian Year* (1993)

Evening

Almighty and everliving God,
in Your tender love for the human race
You sent Your Son our Savior Jesus Christ
to take upon Him our nature, and to suffer death upon the cross,
giving us the example of His great humility:
mercifully grant that we may walk in the way of His suffering,
and also share in His resurrection;
through Jesus Christ our Lord,
who lives and reigns with You and the Holy Spirit, one God,
for ever and ever.
Amen.

—Gelasian Sacramentary (8th c.)

February 26: Lent

Morning

Grant, I beseech Thee, O Lord,
that by the observance of this Lent
I may advance in the knowledge of the mystery of Christ,
and show forth His mind in conduct worthy of my calling;
through Jesus Christ our Lord.
Amen.

—Gelasian Sacramentary (8th c.)

Evening

O God,
who for our redemption gave Your only-begotten Son
to the death of the cross,
and by His glorious resurrection
delivered us from the power of our enemy:
grant us so to die daily to sin,
that we may evermore live with Him in the joy of His resurrection;
who lives and reigns now and forever.
Amen.

—Book of Common Prayer (1979)

February 27: Lent

O Lord, have mercy on me, a sinner.
Establish my heart in Your will.
Grant me true repentance for my sins:
right faith and true charity,
patience in adversity
and moderation in prosperity.
Help me and all my friends and kinsmen,
all who desire and trust in my prayers. . . .
To You, my God. . . . be praise and glory forever
for all the benefits You have given me,
and for all Your mercies to me, a sinner,
for Your name's sake.
Amen.

—Wulfstan (c. 1009–1095)

Evening

O Lord and Master of my life,
give me not a spirit of sloth,
vain curiosity, lust for power and idle talk.
But give to me, Your servant,
a spirit of soberness,
humility, patience and love.
Yea, O Lord and King,
grant me to see my own faults,
and not to condemn my brother;
for blessed are You to the ages of ages.
Amen.

—Ephraim the Syrian (c. 305–373)

February 28: Lent

Morning

I have much need of humbling myself before You,
the great and holy God,
because of the sins that I am daily guilty of in thought, word and deed
against Your divine majesty.
Help me to overcome habitual levity in my thoughts
and to shun vain and impure thoughts which,
though they do not take up their abode in my mind
for any long period of time,
yet, in their passing through, often leave a tincture of impurity.
Enable me to keep my heart with all diligence, my thoughts and affections,
for out of them are the issues of life.
How often have I offended in this kind!
Cleanse me from secret faults, for out of the abundance
of the heart the mouth speaks.
Help me to guard against vain and unnecessary words,
and to speak of You, my God,
with that reverence, that humility, that gravity that I ought.
Amen.

—Susanna Wesley (1669–1742)

Evening

O God,
we belong to You utterly.
You are such a Father
that You take our sins from us
and throw them behind Your back.
You clean our souls
as Your Son also washed the disciples' feet.
We hold up our hearts to You:
make them what they must be.
Amen.

—George MacDonald (1824–1905)

February 29 (Leap Years): Lent

Morning

Good Jesus, my God and my all,
Be Thou all to me,
Be Thou all in me,
That I may be all Thine,
And all Thy will mine.
Make me cheerful under every cross,
For love of Thy cross;
Take from me all which displeases Thee,
Or hinders Thy love in me,
That I may deeply love Thee.
Melt me with Thy love,
That I may be all love,
And with my whole being love Thee.
Good Jesus, who gavest Thyself for me,
Give me of the fullness of Thy love,
That for all Thy love,
With Thy love, I may love Thee.
Amen.

—Edward Bouverie Pusey (1800–1882)

Evening

Make Thou my spirit
Pure and clear
As are the frosty skies,
Or this first snowdrop of the year
That in my bosom lies.
Amen.

—Alfred, Lord Tennyson (1809–1892)

March 1: Lent

Morning

God, I would put my house in order;
Clear out the dry gray cobwebs
Of stale custom that hang thick upon
Window and wall, that choke
Garret and cellar, and let in the sun
Of fearless thought.
I would, remorseless, sweep
Old broken dreams that clutter
Dusty corners, that supinely sleep
Beneath dark recessed eaves, to make
Place for new dreams, staunch, purposeful.
I would wipe out old moldering grief and take
For it clean, golden memories; scour with sand
Of true repentance stains of old sin;
Then fling my door wide, God, and bid You look within.
Amen.

—Edith Mirick (c. 1930)

Evening

O Thou. . . . Thou who are a fire,
consuming the unworthy, consume me not, O my Creator;
but rather pass through all my body parts, into all my joints,
my will, my heart.
Burn Thou the thorns of all my transgressions,
cleanse my soul, and hallow my thoughts.
Enlighten my five senses; establish me wholly in awe of Thee;
ever shelter me, and guard and keep me
from every soul-corrupting deed and word.
Chasten me, purify me, and control me;
adorn me, teach me, and enlighten me.
Amen.

—Simeon Metaphrastes (10th c.)

MARCH 2: LENT

Morning

O Lord,
for Thy mercy's sake,
lay not my sins to my charge,
but forgive that which is past
and give me grace to amend my life,
to decline from sin and incline toward virtue,
that I may walk with a perfect heart before Thee,
now and evermore.
Amen.

—RICHARD FARRANT (1530–1580)

Evening

My God,
I am sorry for my sins with all my heart.
In choosing to do wrong
and failing to do good,
I have sinned against You
whom I should love above all things.
I firmly intend, with Your help,
to do penance,
to sin no more,
and to avoid whatever leads me to sin.
Our Savior Jesus Christ suffered and died for us.
In His name, my God, have mercy.
Amen.

—ACT OF CONTRITION, CATHOLIC PRAYER

Morning

Almighty and Giver of all mercies, Father of all,
who knows my heart and pities its weaknesses:
You know the desire of my soul to do Your will.
It struggles to wing its flight to You, its Creator,
and sinks again in sorrow for that imperfection which draws it back to earth.
How long will I contend with sin and morality . . .
Redeemer of sinners! Who gave Your life to save us,
assist a miserable sinner who strives with the corruption
and desires above all things to break the snares of the enemy.
Amen.

—ELIZABETH ANN SETON (1774–1821)

Evening

O Lord, heavenly Father, by whose divine ordinance
the darkness covers the earth
and brings unto us bodily rest and quietness,
I render Thee my hearty thanks for the loving-kindness
which Thou hast shown in preserving me during the past day,
and in giving me all things necessary for my health and comfort.
And I beseech Thee, for Jesus Christ's sake,
to forgive me all the sins I have committed
in thought, word, or deed,
and that Thou wilt shadow me this night
under the wings of Thy almighty power,
and defend me from all power of the evil one.
May my soul, whether sleeping or waking,
wait upon Thee, delight in Thee, and ever more praise Thee,
so that when the light of day returns,
I may rise with a pure and thankful heart,
casting away the works of darkness,
and putting on the armor of light;
through Jesus Christ.
Amen.

—THOMAS BECON (c. 1512–1567)

March 4: Lent

Morning

Source of Transformation,
my heart begs Your entrance even as it fights and holds You off.
One hand of mine reaches out to You,
but the other hides behind my back,
shunning Your will and Your way for me.
Your coming is not always gentle;
sometimes it sears with painful truth.
While I cry out for You to come, another part of me whispers,
"But not so near as to change me."
When will I freely embrace You?
When will I let go of my old ways? . . .
When will I be vulnerable?
When will I acknowledge my need of You?
When will I learn to give You my all?
Enter and rest in my shadows until they finally give up their dark.
Come, fill my being with Your love,
until Your transforming radiance is the only lasting thing.
Amen.

—Joyce Rupp (1943–)

Evening

God of love, bring me back to You.
Send Your Spirit to make me strong
in faith and active in good works . . .
Father of love, source of all blessings,
help me to pass from my old life of sin
to the new life of grace.
Prepare me for the glory of Your Kingdom.
I ask this through our Lord Jesus Christ, Your Son,
who lives and reigns with You
and the Holy Spirit, one God, forever.
Amen.

—Anonymous Catholic prayer

March 5: Lent

Morning

Lord Jesus,
You are my righteousness;
I am Your sin.
You took on You what was mine;
You set on me what was Yours.
You became what You were not
that I might become what I was not.
Amen.

—Martin Luther (1483–1546)

Evening

How brief is our span of life
compared with the time since You created the universe.
How tiny we are compared with the enormity of Your universe.
How trivial are our concerns
compared with the complexity of Your universe.
How stupid we are compared with the genius of Your creation.
Yet during every minute and every second of our lives
You are present, within and around us.
You give Your whole and undivided attention to each and every one of us.
Our concerns are Your concerns.
And You are infinitely patient with our stupidity.
I thank You with all my heart—
knowing that my thanks are worthless compared with Your greatness.
Amen.

—Fulbert of Chartres (970–1028)

Morning

Lord, hear; Lord, forgive; Lord, do.
Hear what I speak not;
forgive what I speak amiss;
do what I leave undone;
that not according to my word
or my deed, but according to Thy
mercy and truth, all may
issue to Thy glory and the
good of Thy kingdom.
Amen.

—MARIA HARE (1798–1870)

Evening

O my God, Trinity whom I adore,
let me entirely forget myself that I may abide in You,
still and peaceful as if my soul were already in eternity;
let nothing disturb my peace
nor separate me from You, O my unchanging God,
but that each moment may take me
further into the depths of Your mystery.
Amen.

—ELIZABETH OF THE TRINITY (1880–1906)

Morning

Since You came into the world for all people, O Savior,
therefore You came for me, for I am one of the people.
Since You came into the world to save sinners,
therefore You came to save me, for I am one of the sinners.
Since You came to find those who are lost,
therefore You came to find me, for I am one of the lost.
O Lord, O my God and Creator!
I should have come to You as a transgressor of Your law. . . .
But I was so proud and so stubborn that You had to come to me.
You had to come down to earth as a tiny baby,
enduring poverty, discomfort and danger, in order to reach me.
You had to walk dusty lanes, enduring insults and persecution,
in order to reach me.
You had to suffer and die on a cross, in order to reach me.
Forgive me my stubborn pride that I have put You
to such trouble and such pain on my behalf. . . .
I shall offer You thanksgiving, face to face, with Your chosen ones,
and shall sing, and praise, and glorify You,
with the Eternal Father and the Holy Ghost, forever and ever.
Amen.

—TYCHON OF ZADONSK (1724–1783)

Evening

Good Jesus, too late have I loved Thee,
nor ever have I wholly followed Thee;
make me now at last wholly to love Thee,
and out of the fullness of Thine infinite love
give me all the love that I might have had, had I always loved Thee. . . .
O dearest Lord, who art Love,
give me of Thine own love
that therewith I may wholly love Thee.
Amen.

—EDWARD BOUVERIE PUSEY (1800–1882)

MARCH 8: LENT

Morning

Almighty God,
who seest that we have
no power of ourselves
to help ourselves;
keep us both outwardly in
our bodies, and inwardly in
our souls; that we may be defended
from all adversities which may
happen to the body,
and from all evil thoughts which may
assault and hurt the soul:
through Jesus Christ our Lord.
Amen.

—BOOK OF COMMON PRAYER (1928)

Evening

Two things I recognize in myself, Lord:
I am made in Your image;
I have defaced that likeness.
I admit to my fault,
but remember, Lord, by myself I cannot do much about it.
Take from me what I have spoiled;
leave in me what You have made.
Amen.

—LANCELOT ANDREWES (1555–1626)

MARCH 9: LENT

Morning

Dear Lord,
we are now as a church in the holy
Season of Lent. These are days
of salvation, these are the acceptable days.
I know that I am a sinner, that
in many ways I have offended You. I
see that sin withers Your life within
me, as drought withers the leaves
on a tree in the desert.
Help me now, Lord, in my attempt to
turn from sin. Bless my efforts with
the rich blessing of Your grace.
Help me to see that the least thing I do
for You, or give up for You,
will be rewarded by You
"full measure, pressed down,
shaken together and flowing over."
Then I shall see in my own soul
how the desert can blossom, and the dry and wasted land
bring forth the rich, useful fruit which was
expected of it from the beginning.
Amen.

—COUNTRY PRAYER FOR LENT, A TRADITIONAL CATHOLIC PRAYER

Evening

Lord God almighty,
grant me grace to withstand the temptations of the world,
the flesh, and the devil,
and with a pure heart and mind to follow You,
the only God,
through Jesus Christ our Lord.
Amen.

—*ANGLICAN ALTERNATIVE SERVICE BOOK* (1980)

March 10: Lent

Morning

Lamb of God,
You take away the sins of the world:
have mercy on us.
Lamb of God,
You take away the sins of the world:
have mercy on us.
Lamb of God,
You take away the sins of the world:
grant us peace.
Amen.

—Roman Missal

Evening

Lord,
You are to be blessed and praised;
all good things come from You:
You are in our words and in our thoughts,
and in all that we do that is good.
Amen.

—Teresa of Ávila (1515–1582)

MARCH 11: LENT

Morning

Lord Jesus Christ, Son of God,
have mercy on me, a sinner.
Amen.

—ANCIENT EASTERN ORTHODOX PRAYER

Evening

O God, I love Thee, I love Thee—
Not out of hope of heaven for me
Nor fearing not to love and be
In the everlasting burning.
Thou, Thou, my Jesus, after me
Didst reach Thine arms out dying,
For my sake sufferedst nails and lance,
Mocked and marred countenance,
Sorrows passing number,
Sweat and care and cumber,
Yea and death, and this for me,
And Thou couldst see me sinning;
Then I, why should not I love Thee,
Jesus, so much in love with me?
Not for heaven's sake; not to be
Out of hell by loving Thee;
Not for any gains I see;
But just the way that Thou didst me
I do love and I will love Thee:
What must I love Thee, Lord, for then?
For being my king and God. Amen.

—FRANCIS XAVIER (1506–1552); TRANSLATED BY GERARD MANLEY
HOPKINS (1844–1889)

Morning

Grant to me, O Lord,
to know what I ought to know,
to love what I ought to love,
to praise what delights You most,
to value what is precious in Your sight,
to hate what is offensive to You.
Do not suffer me to judge according
to the sight of my eyes
nor to pass sentence according to the
hearing of ignorant men;
but to discern with true judgment
between things visible and spiritual
and above all things to inquire
what is the good pleasure of Your will.
Amen.

—Thomas à Kempis (1380–1471)

Evening

Blessed Father God,
may we show ourselves to be faithful.
Our effort here is brief,
the reward is eternal.
May the excitements of the world
vanish like a shadow,
and not disturb us.
Amen.

—Clare of Assisi (1194–1253)

Morning

How shall I repay Your generosity,
O Lover of my soul?
How shall I repay You for all You
have done for me and given me?
If I had died a thousand times for
Your sake, it would be as nothing . . .
How shall I thank You, who suffered
dishonor, insult, mockery, scourging, and
death for our sakes? . . .
The only thing I can return to You is my prayers,
that time I devote each day
to speaking and listening to You.
Receive my prayer as a tiny token of
my enormous gratitude.
Amen.

—TYCHON OF ZADONSK (1724–1783)

Evening

Heavenly Father,
our Source of life,
I reach out with joy to grasp Your hand!
Let me walk more readily in Your ways.
Guide me in Your gentle mercy,
for left to myself I cannot do Your will.
Father of love,
Source of all blessings,
help me to pass from my old life of sin
to the new life of grace.
Prepare me for the glory of Your kingdom.
I ask this through our Lord Jesus Christ.
Amen.

—LENTEN PRAYER FOR SPIRITUAL RENEWAL

March 14: Lent

Morning

It is Thou who givest the bright sun, together with the ice;
it is Thou who createdst the rivers and the salmon in the river.
That the nut-tree should be flowering, O Christ, it is a rare craft;
through Thy skill too comes the kernel, Thou fair ear of our wheat.
Though the children of Eve ill deserve the bird-flocks and the salmon,
it was the Immortal One on the cross
who made both the salmon and birds.
It is He who makes the flower of the sloe
grow through the bark of the blackthorn,
and the nut-flower on the trees;
beside this, what miracle is greater?
Amen.

—Tadhg Óg Ó Huiginn (Irish poet, d. 1448)

Evening

O Lord,
reassure me with Your quickening Spirit;
without You I can do nothing.
Mortify in me all . . . worldliness, pride,
selfishness, and resistance to God,
and fill me with love, peace,
and all the fruits of the Spirit. . . .
You are the same yesterday, today, and forever;
and therefore, waiting on Thee, Lord,
I trust that I shall at length renew my strength.
Amen.

—William Wilberforce (1759–1833)

MARCH 15: LENT

Morning

As a needle turns to the north when it is touched by the magnet,
so it is fitting, O Lord, that I, Your servant,
should turn to love and praise and serve You;
seeing that out of love to me
You were willing to endure such grievous pangs and sufferings.
Amen.

—RAYMOND LULL (1235–1315)

Evening

O You who are all my hope, all my glory, my sole refuge. . . .
O Life of my soul, Rest of my spirit and its joy!
O fair bright Day of eternity, and evening Light of my inmost being. . . .
O Lord my God, prepare within me a dwelling for Yourself,
that according to the promise of Your holy word,
You may come to me, and abide within me.
Amen.

—PETER OF ALCANTARA (1499–1562)

Morning

Come, my Light, and illumine my darkness.
Come, my Life, and raise me from death.
Come, my Physician, and heal my wounds.
Come, Flame of divine Love, and burn up my sins.
Come, my King, sit upon the throne of my heart and reign there.
For you alone are my King and my Lord.
Amen.

—DIMITRII OF ROSTOV (1651–1709)

Evening

O Holy Spirit, most sweet Comforter . . .
I beseech Thee,
come and glide into my heart.
Wash me over and over, and cleanse me
thoroughly from all sin, and hallow my soul.
Look on my soul, wash its filth,
bedew its drought,
heal its wounds,
bend its stiffness,
warm its chill,
guide its waywardness.
Make me truly humble and resigned
that I may please Thee;
and do Thou ever rest upon me.
O most blessed Light of all loveliness,
be Thou shed on me!
Kindle within me the fire of Thy burning love.
Amen.

—LOUIS DE BLOIS (1506–1566)

March 17: Lent

Morning

I rise today with the power of God to guide me,
the might of God to uphold me,
the wisdom of God to teach me,
the eye of God to watch over me,
the ear of God to hear me,
the word of God to give me speech,
the hand of God to protect me,
the path of God to lie before me,
the shield of God to shelter me,
the host of God to defend me
against the snares of the devil and the temptations of the world,
against every man who meditates injury to me,
whether far or near.
Amen.

—Patrick of Ireland (c. 387–c. 460)

Evening

Guard for me my eyes,
Jesus, Son of Mary,
lest seeing others' wealth make me covetous.
Guard for me my ears,
lest they harken to slander,
lest they listen to folly in the sinful world.
Guard for me my heart,
O Christ, in Thy love,
lest I ponder wretchedly the desire of any iniquity.
Guard for me my hands,
that they be not stretched out for quarreling,
or practice shameful idleness.
Guard for me my feet upon the gentle earth. . . .
lest they be bent on profitless errands.
Amen.

—Ancient Irish prayer

MARCH 18: LENT

Morning

O Lord, in Your great mercy,
keep us from forgetting what You have suffered for us
in body and soul.
May we never be drawn by the cares of this life
from Jesus our Friend and Savior,
but daily may live nearer to His cross.
Amen.

—CAPTAIN HEDLEY VICARS (1826–1855)

Evening

O Thou great Chief of the world,
light a candle in my heart
that I may see what is therein
and sweep the rubbish from my dwelling place.
Amen.

—AFRICAN PRAYER

March 19: Lent

Morning

Father,
all-powerful and ever-living God,
during the holy season of Lent You call
us to a closer union with Yourself.
Help me to prepare to celebrate
the Paschal Mystery with my mind
and my heart renewed. Give me a
spirit of loving reverence for You, our Father,
and a spirit of willing service to my neighbor.
Amen.

—Catholic novena for Lent

Evening

O good Shepherd, seek me, and bring me home to Your fold again. . . .
Deal favorably with me according to Your grace,
till I may dwell in Your house all the days of my life,
and praise You for ever and ever with those who are there.
Amen.

—Jerome (347–420)

MARCH 20: LENT

Morning

My eternal Lord and Father,
I am your poor, unworthy child.
Teach me and make me know,
so that I can observe Your ways.
That is my truest desire.
Amen.

—ANABAPTIST HYMN BY ANNELEIN OF FREIBURG (1512–1529)

Evening

O Good Shepherd Jesus, good, gentle, tender Shepherd . . .
I ask You, by the power of Your most sweet name,
and by Your holy manhood's mystery,
to put away my sins and heal the languors of my soul,
mindful only of Your goodness, not of my ingratitude.
Lord, may Your good, sweet Spirit descend into my heart,
and fashion there a dwelling for Himself.
Amen.

—AELRED OF RIEVAULX (c. 1110–1167)

Morning

Have mercy upon me, O God,
According to Your lovingkindness;
According to the multitude of Your tender mercies,
Blot out my transgressions.
Wash me thoroughly from my iniquity,
And cleanse me from my sin.
For I acknowledge my transgressions,
And my sin is always before me.
Create in me a clean heart, O God,
And renew a steadfast spirit within me.
Do not cast me away from Your presence,
And do not take Your Holy Spirit from me.
Restore to me the joy of Your salvation,
And uphold me by Your generous Spirit.
Amen.

—PSALM 51:1–3, 10–12

Evening

O God, whose glory it is always to have mercy:
be gracious to all who have gone astray from Thy ways,
and bring them again with penitent hearts and steadfast faith
to embrace and hold fast the unchangeable truth of Thy Word,
Jesus Christ Thy Son; who with Thee and the Holy Spirit
liveth and reigneth, one God, for ever and ever.
Amen.

—BOOK OF COMMON PRAYER (1979)

Morning

Stand by me, Lord,
and hold me upright when the gales of sin blow round me.
And when the dark stormy night of wickedness closes in on me,
guide my steps.
My soul is already baffled by the temptations to which I have
    submitted. . . .
The trees around me flourish and spread their branches.
But I am hemmed in by the guilt which surrounds me. . . .
Ah Lord, You are the only remedy.
I accept that while I remain on earth I must endure hardships. . . .
Let my suffering bring me true contrition,
that I may receive Your forgiveness,
and so be made fit for the everlasting joy of Heaven.
Amen.

—THE EXETER BOOK (c. 950)

Evening

Come, Holy Spirit, into my soul,
and help me know my sins.
Help me feel true remorse
and confess them humbly,
that I may enjoy the Father's forgiveness.
By Your light illumine the darkness of my mind;
by Your fire warm my cold heart.
May I realize the wrongs that I have done,
and the good that I failed to do.
Strengthen my determination to avoid these sins in the future,
and to live in Your love, peace, and joy.
Amen.

—ANONYMOUS CATHOLIC PRAYER

MARCH 23: LENT

Morning

Honored Jesus,
You lived a life on earth in which
Your every word was truth,
and every act was one of courage, kindness, and righteousness.
You lived Your life here as a complete Being,
because for You all of life was spiritual.
No portion of Yourself was partitioned off,
beyond the Divine Will.
Lord Jesus, I do love You and most earnestly worship You.
Help me today, please, to be even the palest reflection
of that completeness that was and is Yours.
Then I, like a tiny sliver of glass that glitters in the sunshine,
will reflect back to the world Your godly brightness.
Amen.

—JEANIE GUSHEE (1962–)

Evening

Look down upon me, good and gentle Jesus,
while before Your face I humbly kneel
and with burning soul pray and beseech You
to fix deep in my heart lively sentiments of faith,
hope, and charity, true contrition for my sins,
and a firm purpose of amendment.
I contemplate, with great love, and tender pity,
Your five most precious wounds, pondering over them within me
and calling to mind the words that David, Your prophet,
said of You, my Jesus:
"They have pierced My hands and My feet, they have numbered My bones."
Amen.

—TRADITIONAL CATHOLIC PRAYER

CHRIST'S ENTRY INTO JERUSALEM

MARCH 24: PALM SUNDAY

Morning

Ride on! Ride on in majesty!
Hark! All the tribes "Hosanna" cry;
Thine humble beast pursues his road,
With palms and scattered garments strewed.
Ride on! Ride on in majesty!
In lovely pomp ride on to die:
O Christ, Thy triumphs now begin
O'er captive death and conquered sin.
Ride on! Ride on in majesty!
The winged squadrons of the sky
Look down with sad and wondering eyes
To see the approaching Sacrifice . . .
Amen.

—DEAN HENRY MILMAN (1791–1868)

Evening

Let the mountains and all the hills
break out into great rejoicing at the mercy of God,
and let the trees of the forest clap their hands.
Give praise to Christ, all nations,
magnify Him, all peoples, crying:
Glory to Thy power, O Lord.
Seated in heaven upon Thy throne
and on earth upon a foal, O Christ our God,
Thou hast accepted the praise of the angels,
and the songs of the children who cried out to Thee:
Blessed are Thou that comest to call back Adam.
Amen.

—EASTERN ORTHODOX PRAYER

Morning

O Christ, the King of glory,
who didst enter the holy city in meekness,
to be made perfect through the suffering of death:
give me grace, I beseech Thee, in all
my life here to take up my cross daily
and follow Thee,
that hereafter I may rejoice with Thee
in Thy heavenly kingdom;
who livest and reignest with the Father and the Holy Spirit,
God, world without end.
Amen.

—CHURCH OF SOUTH INDIA

Evening

O Lord Jesus,
help me.
Strengthen my faith and trust in You.
In You I have sealed all the treasures I have.
I am poor; You are rich,
and came to be merciful to the poor.
I am a sinner; You are upright.
With me there is an abundance of sin;
in You is the fullness of righteousness.
Therefore I will remain with You,
from whom I can receive,
but to whom I can give nothing.
Amen.

—MARTIN LUTHER (1483–1546)

Morning

You taught us, Lord, that the greatest love a man
can show is to lay down his life for his friends.
But Your love was greater still, because You laid
down Your life for Your enemies. It was while
we were still enemies that You reconciled us
to Yourself by Your death.
What other love has ever been,
or could ever be, like Yours?
You suffered unjustly for the sake of the unjust.
You died at the hands of sinners
for the sake of the sinful.
You became a slave to tyrants,
to set the oppressed free.
Amen.

—BERNARD OF CLAIRVAUX (1090–1153)

Evening

Soul of Christ, sanctify me.
Body of Christ, save me.
Blood of Christ, inebriate me.
Water from the side of Christ, wash me.
Passion of Christ, strengthen me.
O Good Jesus, hear me.
Within Your wounds hide me;
separated from You may I never be.
From the malignant enemy defend me.
At the hour of my death call me,
and close to You bid me,
that with Your saints I may praise You
for all eternity.
Amen.

—*ANIMA CHRISTI*, ANONYMOUS (14TH C.)

March 27: Wednesday of Holy Week

Morning

I have gathered pearls together to make a crown for the Son
in place of my sinful body.
Receive my offering, although You lack nothing;
I offer it because of my own lack. Whiten my stains!
This crown is made of spiritual pearls,
which are set in love, not in gold,
clasped in a mounting of faith;
let our praise be the hands that offer it to God!
Amen.

—Ephraim the Syrian (c. 305–373)

Evening

O Lord Jesus, who came down from heaven
to redeem us from all iniquity,
we beseech You to write Your word in our hearts
that we may know You,
and the power of Your resurrection,
and express it in turning from our sins.
Rule in our hearts by faith,
that being dead to sin and living to righteousness,
we may bear the fruit of holiness
and grow in grace and in personal knowledge of You.
Amen.

—Henry Hammond (1605–1660)

March 28: Maundy Thursday

Morning

Gracious God, who does, with the most inestimable gift of Your love,
freely give all things which we need,
O give me more and more the lovely ornament of humility!
Enable me to meditate with delightful attention
on the excellencies of my Saviour
and ardently desire to be more like Him in this engaging virtue! . . .
Did He not even stoop to wash the feet of His disciples,
to teach them a lesson of affectionate humility!
And shall not I, a poor sinful creature, rejoice to be able
to administer any comfort or assistance to the meanest of His servants?
Transform me, blessed Saviour, into Your own lovely image,
and make me meek and lowly.
Amen.

—Anne Steele (1717–1778)

Evening

O Jesus—
on that very last night
You simply asked us to love one another.
One last session with Your followers;
Your own cruel death just hours away;
there was so much You could have said.
But what You did say was: Love one another.
As I have loved you, you must love one another.
You said: After I am gone, the world will know
that you are My followers
if you love one another.
In remembrance of You,
may we love one another.
Amen.

—David P. Gushee (1962–)

LAST SUPPER

Morning

O Jesus, poor and abject, unknown and despised, have mercy upon me,
and let me not be ashamed to follow Thee.
O Jesus, hated, calumniated, and persecuted, have mercy upon me,
and make me content to be as my master.
O Jesus, blasphemed, accused, and wrongfully condemned,
have mercy upon me,
and teach me to endure the contradictions of sinners.
O Jesus, clothed with a habit of reproach and shame, have mercy upon me,
and let me not seek my own glory.
O Jesus, insulted, mocked, and spit upon, have mercy upon me,
and let me not faint in fiery trial.
O Jesus, crowned with thorn and hailed in derision;
O Jesus, burdened with our sins and the curses of people;
O Jesus, affronted, outraged, buffeted,
overwhelmed with injuries, griefs and humiliations;
O Jesus, hanging on the accursed tree, bowing the head,
giving up the ghost, have mercy upon me,
and conform my whole soul to Thy holy, humble, suffering Spirit.
Amen.

—JOHN WESLEY (1703–1791)

Evening

We implore You,
by the memory of Your cross's hallowed and most bitter anguish,
make us fear You, make us love You, O Christ.
Amen.

—BRIDGET OF KILDARE (453–523)

CRUCIFIXION

March 30: Holy Saturday

Morning

O Jesus,
I devotedly embrace that honored cross
where Thou didst love us even unto death.
In that death I place all my confidence.
Henceforth let me live only for Thee;
and let me die loving Thee, and in Thy sacred arms.
Amen.

—Richard Challoner (1691–1781)

Evening

O Thou Prince of Peace,
who, when Thou was reviled, reviledst not again,
and on the Cross didst pray for Thy murderers:
implant in our hearts the virtues of gentleness, and patience,
that we may overcome evil with good,
for Thy sake love our enemies,
and as children of our heavenly Father seek Thy peace
and evermore rejoice in Thy love.
Amen.

—*Treasury of Devotion* (1876)

RESURRECTION

Morning

Christ the Lord is risen today, Alleluia!
Sons of men and angels say: Alleluia!
Raise Your joys and triumphs high, Alleluia!
Sing, ye heavens, and earth reply: Alleluia!
Lives again our glorious King, Alleluia!
Where, O death, is now Thy sting? Alleluia!
Dying once, He all doth save, Alleluia!
Where thy victory, O grave? Alleluia!
Love's redeeming work is done, Alleluia!
Fought the fight, the battle won, Alleluia!
Death in vain forbids Him rise, Alleluia!
Christ has opened Paradise, Alleluia!
Amen.

—CHARLES WESLEY (1707–1788)

Evening

The moment we have longed for has come;
the night of our desires is here!
What greater occupation could there be
than for us to proclaim the power of Your resurrection!
This was the day when You shattered the gates of hell,
and You took up the victory banner of Heaven.
This was the day when You set us among the stars. . . .
The blood which flowed from Your side has washed away our sins.
Your body rising from the tomb has promised us eternal life.
Eternal are the blessings which in Your love You have poured upon us!
Amen.

—GELASIAN SACRAMENTARY (8TH C.)

April 1: Monday of Easter Week

Morning

Christ is risen: the world below lies desolate.
Christ is risen: the spirits of evil are fallen.
Christ is risen: the angels of God are rejoicing.
Christ is risen: the tombs of the dead are empty.
Christ is risen indeed from the dead, the first of the sleepers.
Glory and power are His forever and ever.
Amen.

—Hippolytus of Rome (c. 190–c. 236)

Evening

It is truly right and good, always and everywhere,
with our whole heart and mind and voice,
to praise You, the invisible, almighty, and eternal God,
and Your only-begotten Son, Jesus Christ our Lord;
for He is the true Paschal Lamb, who at the feast of the Passover
paid for us the debt of Adam's sin,
and by His blood delivered Your faithful people....
How wonderful and beyond our knowing,
O God, is Your mercy and loving-kindness to us,
that to redeem a slave, You gave a Son.
Amen.

—Book of Common Prayer (1979; translation
of Latin Liturgy, 6th c.)

Morning

Lord, You have passed over into new life,
and You now invite us to pass over also.
In these past days we have grieved at Your suffering
and mourned at Your death.
We have given ourselves over to repentance and prayer,
to abstinence and gravity.
Now at Easter You tell us that we have died to sin.
Yet, if this is so, how can we remain on earth?
How can we pass over to Your risen life, while we are still in this world?
Will we not be just as meddlesome, just as lazy, just as selfish as before?
Will we not still be bad-tempered and stubborn,
enmeshed in all the vices of the past?
I pray that as we pass over with You, our faces will never look back.
Instead, let us, like You, make Heaven on earth.
Amen.

—BERNARD OF CLAIRVAUX (1090–1153)

Evening

Rejoice, heavenly powers!
Sing, choirs of angels!
Exalt, all creation around God's throne!
Jesus Christ, our King, is risen!
Sound the trumpet of salvation!
Rejoice, O Earth, in shining splendor,
Radiant in the brightness of your King!
Christ has conquered!
Glory fills you!
Darkness vanishes for ever!
Amen.

—EXSULTET (6TH c.)

April 3: Wednesday of Easter Week

Morning

You have protected us, Jesus, from endless disaster.
You spread Your hands over us like wings.
You poured Your blood over the earth, because You loved us.
The anger which we deserved You turned away from us,
and restored us to friendship with God.
The Heavens may have Your spirit, Paradise Your soul,
but the earth has Your blood.
We celebrate the coming of Your Spirit always:
the Spirit leads the mystic dance throughout the year.
But Easter comes and goes.
Power came from Heaven to raise You from death,
so that we and all creatures could see You.
All living things gather round You at Easter.
There is joy, honor, celebration, and delight!
Amen.

—Hippolytus of Rome (c. 190–c. 236)

Evening

O Death, where is thy sting? O Hades, where is thy pride?
Christ is risen, and thou art abolished!
Christ is risen, and the demons are fallen.
Christ is risen, and the angels rejoice.
Christ is risen, and the life reigns. . . .
For Christ, who rose from the dead,
has become the leader and the reviver
of those who have fallen asleep.
To Him be glory and dominion unto ages of ages!
Amen.

—John Chrysostom (c. 347–407)

Morning

We have seen the resurrection of the Christ!
I worship You, holy Jesus, who alone are without sin!
I praise You and glorify Your Holy Resurrection.
For You alone are our God;
I know no other, save for You.
Upon Your name I call.
I, one of Your faithful ones, adore the Holy Resurrection of our Lord,
for through Your cross joy has come to all the world!
Ever blessing You, O Lord,
I sing praises of Your Resurrection.
You endured the cross on our behalf,
and have destroyed death by death.
Amen.

—EASTERN ORTHODOX LITURGY

Evening

Almighty God,
who through the death of Your Son has destroyed sin and death,
and by His resurrection has restored innocence and everlasting life,
that we may be delivered from the dominion of the devil,
and our mortal bodies raised up from the dead:
grant that I may confidently and wholeheartedly believe this,
and, finally, with Your saints,
share in the joyful resurrection of the just;
through the same Jesus Christ, Your Son, our Lord.
Amen.

—MARTIN LUTHER (1483–1546)

APRIL 5: FRIDAY OF EASTER WEEK

Morning

Glory to You, Lord Jesus Christ! You built Your cross as a bridge over death,
so that departed souls might pass from the realm of death to the realm of life.
Glory to You! You put on the body of a mortal man
and made it the source of life for all mortal human beings.
You are alive! Your murderers handled Your life like farmers:
they sowed it like grain deep in the earth,
for it to spring up and raise with itself a multitude of men.
We offer You the great, universal sacrifice of our love,
and pour out before You our richest hymns and prayers.
For You offered Your cross to God as a sacrifice
in order to make us all rich.
Amen.

—EPHRAIM THE SYRIAN (c. 305–373)

Evening

I see flames of orange, yellow, and red
Shooting upwards to the sky,
Piercing the whole clouds.
I see the clouds themselves
Chasing the flames upwards,
And I feel the air itself
Reaching for the Heavens.
Down below I see great, grey rocks
Beating against the earth,
As if they were pushing their way
Down to hell.
At Your resurrection that which is light and good
Rises up with You,
And that which is heavy and evil is pushed downwards.
At Your resurrection goodness breaks from evil,
Life breaks free from death.
Amen.

—ADAM OF ST. VICTOR (12TH c.)

April 6: Saturday of Easter Week

Morning

O glorious resurrection!
God of Abraham and all our Fathers,
in all the centuries during which the believers
have placed their hope in Thee,
none has ever been deceived.
Therefore my hope also is in Thee.
Amen.

—Ida Calvin (1505–1549)

Evening

At the Lamb's high feast we sing
Praise to our victorious King,
Who hath washed us in the tide
Flowing from His pierced side. . . .
Mighty Victim from the sky,
Hell's fierce powers beneath Thee lie;
Thou hast conquered in the fight,
Thou hast brought us life and light;
Now no more can death appall,
Now no more the grave enthrall;
Thou hast opened paradise,
and in Thee Thy saints shall rise.
Paschal triumph, Paschal joy,
Sin alone can this destroy;
From sin's power do Thou set free
Souls new-born, O Lord, in Thee.
Hymns of glory, songs of praise,
Father, unto Thee we raise:
Risen Lord, all praise to Thee
With the Spirit ever be.
Amen.

—Latin hymn (1632); translated by Robert Campbell (1849)

Morning

As I rejoice in the gift of this new day,
so may the light of Your presence, O God,
set my heart on fire with love for You,
now and for ever.
Amen.

—THE DIVINE OFFICE

Evening

I adore, I venerate, I glory in that cross, which You represent to us,
and by that cross I adore our merciful Lord,
and what He has in mercy done for us! . . .
By You, hell is spoiled; its mouth is closed to the redeemed.
By You, demons are afraid, restrained and defeated.
By You, the whole world is renewed and made beautiful.
Amen.

—ANSELM OF CANTERBURY (1033–1109)

APRIL 8

Morning

I take God the Father to be my God;
I take God the Son to be my Savior;
I take God the Holy Ghost to be my Sanctifier;
I take the Word of God to be my rule;
I take the people of God to be my people;
and I do hereby dedicate and yield my whole self to the Lord:
and I do this deliberately, freely, and for ever.
Amen.

—MATTHEW HENRY (1662–1714)

Evening

O Heart of Jesus, treasure of tenderness,
You Yourself are my happiness, my only hope.
You who knew how to charm my tender youth,
stay near me till the last light.
Lord, to You I have given my life,
and all my desires are well known to You.
It's in Your ever infinite goodness that I want to lose myself,
O Heart of Jesus.
Amen.

—THÉRÈSE OF LISIEUX (1873–1897)

APRIL 9

Morning

O Lord our God, . . .
bless my coming in and my going out,
my thoughts, words, and works,
and let me begin this day with the
praise of the unspeakable sweetness of Thy mercy.
Hallowed be Thy name.
Thy kingdom come;
through Jesus Christ our Lord.
Amen.

—GREEK LITURGY (3RD C.)

Evening

Now I lay me down to sleep,
I pray the Lord my soul to keep.
May angels watch me through the night,
And wake me with the morning light.
Amen.

—ANONYMOUS; TRADITIONAL CHILDREN'S PRAYER

Morning

The prayers I make will then be sweet indeed,
If Thou the Spirit give by which I pray;
My unassisted heart is barren clay,
Which of its native self can nothing feed;
Of good and pious works Thou art the seed
Which quickens where Thou sayest it may;
Unless Thou show to us Thine own true way,
No man can find it! Father, Thou must lead!
Do Thou, then, breathe those thoughts into my mind
By which such virtue may in me be bred
That in Thy holy footsteps I may tread:
The fetters of my tongue do Thou unbind,
That I may have the power to sing of Thee
And sound Thy praises everlastingly.
Amen.

—Michelangelo (1475–1564); translated by William
Wordsworth (1770–1850)

Evening

Lighten my darkness, I beseech Thee, O Lord. . . .
Lord Christ, Your saints have been the lights of the world
in every generation:
grant that I who follow in their footsteps
may be made worthy to enter with them
into that heavenly country where You live and reign for ever and ever.
Amen.

—Book of Common Prayer (1979)

April 11

Morning

O Lord, prepare me for all the events of the day;
for I know not what a day may bring forth.
Give me grace to deny myself;
to take up my cross daily,
and to follow in the steps of my Lord and Master.
Amen.

—Matthew Henry (1662–1714)

Evening

O heavenly Father,
preserve me from all cold and speculative views
of Thy blessed Gospel;
and while with regular constancy I kneel down daily before Thee,
do not fail to light up the fire
of heavenly love in my bosom,
and to draw my heart heavenward
with earnest longings to Thyself.
Amen.

—Henry Kirke White (1785–1806)

Morning

Lord, what is my confidence that I have in this life?
Or what is the greatest comfort I can derive
from anything under heaven?
Is it not Thou, O Lord, whose mercies are without number?
Where hath it ever been well with me without Thee?
Or when could it be ill with me when Thou wert present?
I had rather be poor for Thee, than rich without Thee.
I rather choose to be a pilgrim on earth with Thee
than without Thee to possess heaven.
Where Thou art, there is heaven,
and where Thou art not there is death and hell. . . .
Thou therefore art the End of all that is good,
the Height of Life,
the Depth of all that can be spoken;
and to hope in Thee above all things
is the strongest comfort of Thy servants.
Amen.

—THOMAS À KEMPIS (1380–1471)

Evening

Hear me, Lord, Holy Father,
almighty and eternal God,
and graciously send Your holy angel from heaven
to watch over, to cherish, to protect,
to abide with, and to defend all who dwell in this house;
through Jesus Christ our Lord.
Amen.

—TRADITIONAL CATHOLIC PRAYER

April 13

Morning

Eternal God,
who committest to us the swift and solemn trust of life;
since I know not what a day may bring forth,
but only that the hour for serving Thee is always present,
may I wake to the instant claims of Thy holy will;
not waiting for tomorrow, but yielding today.
In all things draw me to the mind of Christ, that . . .
Thou mayest own me as at one with Him and Thee.
Amen.

—James Martineau (1805–1900)

Evening

On going to bed:
let me be mindful of Thy Name,
O Lord, in the night,
and keep Thy law.
Let my evening prayer ascend to Thee,
and Thy Mercy descend to me;
Thou that givest songs in the night;
that makest the outgoings of the morning
and evening to praise Thee;
that givest to Thy beloved the sleep of health.
Amen.

—Lancelot Andrewes (1555–1626)

April 14

Morning

O sweet and loving God,
When I stay asleep too long,
Oblivious to all Your many blessings,
Then, please, wake me up,
And sing to me Your joyful song.
It is a song without noise or notes.
It is a song of love beyond words,
Of faith beyond the power of human telling.
I can hear it in my soul,
When You awaken me to Your presence.
Amen.

—Mechthild of Magdeburg (c. 1207–c. 1290)

Evening

O Lord my God,
night reminds me that though You do not sleep,
I must.
Night reminds me that You are most certainly God
and I most certainly am not.
The world will carry on without me while I rest—
but without Your sustaining love every moment,
all would be lost.
I have sought to serve You this day.
Where I have failed,
please call it to mind
for my honest confession
and Your kind forgiveness.
May sleep come easily to me tonight.
Amen.

—David P. Gushee (1962–)

Morning

O my God,
make me happy this day in Thy service.
Let me do nothing,
say nothing,
desire nothing,
which is contrary to Thy will.
Give me a thankful spirit,
and a heart full of praise for all
that Thou hast given me,
and for all Thou hast withheld from me.
Amen.

—Ashton Oxenden (1808–1892)

Evening

O Lord our God,
what sins I have this day committed in word, deed, or thought,
forgive me, for You are gracious and You love all people.
Grant me peaceful and undisturbed sleep,
send me Your guardian angel to protect and guard me from every evil,
for You are the guardian of our souls and bodies
and to You I ascribe glory,
to the Father and the Son and the Holy Ghost,
now and for ever and unto the ages of ages.
Amen.

—Russian Orthodox prayer

April 16

Morning

Let Thy word live abundantly among us—
Thy word, the true, the deep,
Thy word, the tender, the loving.
Let it resound; let it ring,
now in speech, now in song
in every house that is called by Thy name. . . .
Holy Spirit, be our guest.
Blow through our souls
as when the mild winds of spring kiss the earth.
Light up our spirits as when the rosy dawn
breaks through the gloom and darkness of the night.
Let every dry and withered heart be refreshed
by the dew Thou sendest from Heaven;
Thou, our Father, Lord, hear our prayer.
Amen.

—Ditlev Gothard Monrad (1811–1887)

Evening

May the Lord be blessed for ever for the great gifts
that He has continually heaped upon me,
and may all that He has created praise Him.
Amen.

—Teresa of Ávila (1515–1582)

APRIL 17

Morning

Teach me, O Father,
how to ask Thee each moment, silently, for Thy help. . . .
If I am disquieted, enable me, by Thy grace,
quickly to turn to Thee.
May nothing this day come between me and Thee.
May I will, do, and say,
just what Thou, my loving and tender Father,
willest me to will, do and say.
Amen.

—EDWARD BOUVERIE PUSEY (1800–1882)

Evening

O gracious Light,
pure brightness of the everliving Father in heaven,
O Jesus Christ, holy and blessed!
Now as we come to the setting of the sun,
and our eyes behold the vesper light,
we sing Thy praises, O God: Father, Son, and Holy Spirit.
Thou art worthy at all times to be praised by happy voices,
O Son of God, O Giver of life, and to be glorified through all the worlds.
Amen.

—*PHOS HILARON* (LATIN HYMN, 4TH C.)

Morning

Fairest Lord Jesus, Ruler of all nature,
O Thou of God and man the Son,
Thee will I cherish, Thee will I honor,
Thou, my soul's glory, joy and crown.
Fair are the meadows, fairer still the woodlands,
Robed in the blooming garb of spring:
Jesus is fairer, Jesus is purer
Who makes the woeful heart to sing.
Fair is the sunshine, fairer still the moonlight,
And all the twinkling starry host:
Jesus shines brighter, Jesus shines purer
Than all the angels heaven can boast.
Beautiful Savior! Lord of all nations!
Son of God and Son of Man!
Glory and honor, praise, adoration,
Now and forever more be Thine.
Amen.

—Anonymous, German (17th c.)

Evening

Lord Jesus Christ, I offer You this night's repose
in union with the eternal repose You have in the bosom of the Father. . . .
I offer You every breath which I shall draw this night
and every motion of my heart as so many acts of love,
praise, adoration, joy, thanksgiving and homage
which will be paid to You in heaven.
I unite myself with . . . all the angels and saints
who will love and glorify You
during this night and throughout all eternity.
Amen.

—Loreto Manual

Morning

Come, O Love, O God, Thou alone art all my love in verity.
Thou art my dearest Salvation, all my hope and my joy,
my supreme and surpassing Good.
In the morning I will stand before Thee, my God,
and will contemplate Thee, my dearest Love,
because Thou art pure delightsomeness and sweetness eternal.
Thou art the thirst of my heart; Thou art all the sufficiency of my spirit.
The more I taste Thee, the more I hunger;
the more I drink, the more I thirst.
Amen.

—GERTRUDE THE GREAT (1256–c. 1302)

Evening

Yours, O Lord, is the day, Yours also is the night;
cover our sins with Your mercy
as You cover the earth with darkness;
and grant that the Son of Righteousness
may always shine in our hearts,
to chase away the darkness of all evil thoughts;
through Jesus Christ our Lord.
Amen.

—ANONYMOUS

Morning

My God,
my life is an instant,
an hour which passes by;
my life is a moment
which I have no power to stay.
You know, O my God,
that to love You here on earth—
I have only today.
Amen.

—THÉRÈSE OF LISIEUX (1873–1897)

Evening

Dear God,
the beauty of Your world is all around me this night:
in the cool, soft air,
in the trills and croaks of tree frogs,
in the twinkling diamond-gleaming stars.
The darkness of night seems to hide
a myriad of small creatures
intent on secret business.
As my day winds down I praise You,
who give a home, a task, and a livelihood
to the smallest of Your creatures,
and have given me this home,
and the tasks and provision that await me tomorrow.
Thank You that as I sleep,
and the night creatures call and scurry,
You do not sleep, but watch over all
with proud parental love.
You are all good in essence;
I know it!
Your good love is the most beautiful part of Your world!
Amen.

—JEANIE GUSHEE (1962–)

APRIL 21

Morning

I thank You God for this most amazing
day: for the leaping greenly spirits of trees
and a blue true dream of sky; and for everything
which is natural which is infinite which is yes
(i who have died am alive again today,
and this is the sun's birthday; this is the birth
day of life and love and wings: and of the gay
great happening illimitably earth)
how should tasting touching hearing seeing
breathing any-lifted from the no
of all nothing-human merely being
doubt unimaginable You?
(now the ears of my ears awake and
now the eyes of my eyes are opened)
Amen.

—E. E. CUMMINGS (1894–1962)

Evening

Remove all worrisome thoughts from my mind,
and let me sleep undisturbed while You watch over me.
Bless all Your people far and near,
and give healing and strength to the sick.
If I have grieved anyone today, forgive me;
if I have offended You, gracious Savior, blot out these sins;
if I have been neglectful and thoughtless, make me different tomorrow.
Protect all Your children from want and worry,
from bitterness and resentment, from strife and anger.
Keep us all in steadfast faith,
and give me grace to resist every temptation to sin.
Keep me humble and pure in heart.
Hear my prayer, almighty Savior and Friend.
Amen.

—*MY PRAYER BOOK* (1980)

Morning

As the hand is made for holding and the eye for seeing,
You have created me for joy, O God.
Share with me in finding that joy everywhere:
in the violet's beauty, in the lark's melody,
in the child's face, in a mother's love,
in the purity of Jesus.
Amen.

—Traditional Scottish Gaelic prayer

Evening

Almighty God, we give You thanks for surrounding us,
as daylight fades, with the brightness of Your vesper light;
and we implore You of Your great mercy that,
as You enfold us with the radiance of this light, so You would
shine into our hearts the brightness of Your Holy Spirit;
through Jesus Christ our Lord.
Amen.

—Ambrosian Sacramentary (5th c.)

April 23

Morning

My soul hath desired Thee all night,
O eternal wisdom!
And in the early morning I turn to Thee
from the depths of my heart.
May Thy holy presence remove
all dangers from my soul and body.
May Thy many graces
fill the inmost recesses of my heart,
and inflame it with Thy divine love.
Amen.

—HENRY SUSO (1295–1366)

Evening

Give us a thankful sense of the blessings in which we live,
of the many comforts of our lot;
that we may not deserve to lose them by discontent or indifference.
Be gracious to our necessities, and guard us,
and all we love, from evil this night. . . .
Above all other blessings, O God, for ourselves, and our fellow-creatures,
we implore Thee to quicken our sense of Thy mercy
in the redemption of the world,
of the value of that holy religion in which we have been brought up,
that we may not, by our own neglect,
throw away the salvation Thou hast given us,
nor be Christians only in name.
Hear us, Almighty God, for His sake who has redeemed us.
Amen.

—JANE AUSTEN (1775–1817)

Morning

O Lord,
in confidence of Thy great mercy and goodness . . .
I most humbly implore the grace and assistance of the Holy Spirit
to enable me to become every day better.
Grant me the wisdom and understanding to know my duty,
and the heart and the will to do it.
Endue me, O Lord, with the true fear and love of Thee,
and with a prudent zeal for Thy glory.
Increase in me the graces of charity and meekness,
of truth and justice,
of humility and patience,
and a firmness of spirit to bear every condition
with constancy and equality of mind.
Amen.

—KING WILLIAM III (1650–1702)

Evening

O Lord God,
the life of mortals, the light of the faithful,
the strength of those who labor, the repose of the dead;
grant me a tranquil night, free from all disturbances;
that after an interval of quiet sleep I may,
by Thy bounty,
at the return of light, be endued with activity from the Holy Spirit,
and . . . render thanks to Thee,
through Jesus Christ our Lord.
Amen.

—MOZARABIC LITURGY (7TH C.)

Morning

O Lord, bright as is the sun, and the sky and the clouds;
green as are the leaves and the fields;
sweet as is the singing of the birds;
we know that they are not all,
and we will not take up with a part for the whole.
They proceed from a center of love and goodness, which is Thee Thyself;
but they are not Thy fullness; they speak of heaven,
but they are not heaven;
they are but as stray beams and dim reflections of Thine image;
they are but the crumbs from the table.
Shine forth, O Lord, as when on Thy Nativity
Thy angels visited the shepherds;
let Thy glory blossom forth as bloom and foliage on the trees.
Amen.

—CARDINAL JOHN HENRY NEWMAN (1801–1890)

Evening

O God, whose greatness knows no limits,
whose wisdom no bounds,
whose peace excels all understanding;
You who love and help us beyond measure—help us to love You.
Though we cannot fully do so because of Your infinite goodness,
increase and deepen our understanding
so that we may love You more and more;
through Jesus Christ our Lord.
Amen.

—BERNARD OF CLAIRVAUX (1090–1153)

Morning

Let me love Thee
so that the honor, riches, and pleasures of the world
may seem unworthy even of hatred—
may be not even encumbrances.
Amen.

—COVENTRY PATMORE (1823–1896)

Evening

Grant me Your evening blessing.
Rock my spirit into peacefulness.
Ease my cares away from me. . . .
As I gaze back upon the day
that I have just traveled with You,
accept my gratitude for the joys
and my sorrow for the failings.
Abiding Peace, bestow upon me,
and upon all who dwell on earth:
Your protective shelter in our sleep,
Your guarding presence from all harm,
Your perceptive Spirit in our dreams.
First Star of the Evening,
be the strong light in my heart.
Shine brightly while I slumber.
Abide with me in tender vigilance
so that I will arise in the morning
with my soul awakened in Your love.
Amen.

—JOYCE RUPP (1943–)

Morning

O God,
from whom I have received life,
and all earthly blessings,
vouchsafe to give unto me each day what I need.
Give unto me strength to perform faithfully
my appointed tasks;
bless the work of my hands and of my mind. . . .
Sanctify my joys and my trials,
and give me grace to seek first Thy kingdom
and its righteousness,
in the sure and certain faith that all else
shall be added unto me;
through Jesus Christ, Thy Son, our Lord and Saviour.
Amen.

—EUGENE BERSIER (1831–1889)

Evening

Lord,
behold my family here assembled.
I thank Thee for this place in which we dwell;
for the love that unites us;
for the peace accorded us this day;
for the hope with which we expect the morrow;
for the health, the work, the food,
and the bright skies, that make our life delightful;
for our friends in all parts of the earth. . . .
Give us courage, gaiety, and the quiet mind.
Amen.

—ROBERT LOUIS STEVENSON (1850–1894)

APRIL 28

Morning

O My God,
since Thou art with me,
and I must now, in obedience to Thy commands,
apply my mind to these outward things,
I beseech Thee to grant me the grace
to continue in Thy presence;
and to this end do Thou prosper me with Thy assistance,
receive all my work
and possess all my affections.
Amen.

—BROTHER LAWRENCE (1611–1691)

Evening

Grant us Thy peace, Lord,
Through the coming night;
Turn Thou for us its
Darkness into light.
From harm and danger
Keep Thy children free,
For dark and light are
Both alike to Thee.
Amen.

—JOHN ELLERTON (1826–1893)

Morning

For the beauty of the earth,
For the glory of the skies;
For the love which from our birth,
Over and around us lies;
Lord of all, to Thee we raise
This, our hymn of grateful praise.
For the wonder of each hour,
Of the day and of the night;
Hill and vale and tree and flow'r,
Sun and moon, and stars of light;
Lord of all, to Thee we raise,
This, our hymn of grateful praise. . . .
For the joy of human love,
Brother, sister, parent, child;
Friends on earth and friends above,
For all gentle thoughts and mild;
Lord of all, to Thee we raise
This, our hymn of grateful praise.
Amen.

—FOLLIOTT S. PIERPOINT (1835–1917)

Evening

Now that the day has ended,
I thank You, Lord,
and I ask that the evening and night be sinless and undisturbed.
Grant this to me, O Savior, and save me.
Amen.

—EASTERN ORTHODOX PRAYER

Morning

Be Thou a light unto mine eyes, music to mine ears,
sweetness to my taste, and a full contentment to my heart.
Be Thou my sunshine in the day, my food at the table, . . .
my clothing in nakedness, and my succour in all necessities.
Lord Jesus, I give Thee my body, my soul, my substance, my fame,
my friends, my liberty, and my life.
Dispose of me and of all that is mine, as it seemeth best to Thee
and to the glory of Thy blessed name.
Amen.

—JOHN COSIN (1594–1672)

Evening

Be Thou a bright flame before me,
Be Thou a guiding star above me,
Be Thou a smooth path below me, . . .
Be Thou a kindly shepherd behind me,
Today—tonight—and forever.
Amen.

—COLUMBA OF IRELAND (c. 521–597)

May 1

Morning

God, guide me with Thy wisdom;
God, chastise me with Thy justice;
God, help me with Thy mercy;
God, protect me with Thy strength;
God, shield me with Thy shade;
God, fill me with Thy grace,
for the sake of Thine anointed Son.
Amen.

—Ancient Scottish prayer

Evening

Continue Thy gracious protection to me, Lord,
this night. Defend me from all dangers,
and from the fear of them,
that I may enjoy such refreshing sleep
as may fit me for the duties of the coming day.
And grant me grace always to live
so close to Thee that I may
never be afraid to die,
so that, living or dying,
I may be completely Thine,
in Jesus Christ our Lord.
Amen.

—Edmund Gibson (1669–1748)

MAY 2

Morning

O God,
who art the unsearchable abyss of peace, the ineffable sea of love,
the fountain of blessings and the bestower of affection,
who sendest peace to those that receive it;
open to me this day the sea of Thy love
and water me with plenteous streams from the riches of Thy grace
and from the most sweet springs of Thy kindness.
Make me a child of quietness and an heir of peace;
enkindle in me the fire of Thy love;
sow in me Thy fear; strengthen my weakness by Thy power;
bind me closely to Thee . . .
in a firm and indissoluble bond of unity.
Amen.

—Syrian Clementine Liturgy (4th c.)

Evening

Lord Jesus Christ,
You are the gentle moon and the joyful stars,
that watch over the darkest night.
You are the source of all peace,
reconciling the whole universe to the Father.
You are the source of all rest, calming troubled hearts,
and bringing sleep to weary bodies.
You are the sweetness that fills our minds with quiet joy,
and can turn the worst nightmares into dreams of heaven.
May I dream of Your sweetness,
rest in Your arms, be at one with Your Father,
and be comforted in the knowledge that You always watch over me.
Amen.

—Erasmus (1466–1536)

MAY 3

Morning

Give me, O Lord, I pray Thee,
firm faith, unwavering hope,
perfect charity.
Pour into my heart
the spirit of wisdom and understanding,
the spirit of counsel and spiritual strength,
the spirit of knowledge and true godliness,
and the spirit of Thy holy fear.
Light eternal, shine in my heart:
Power eternal, deliver me from evil:
Wisdom eternal, scatter the darkness of my ignorance:
Might eternal, pity me.
Amen.

—ALCUIN OF YORK (c. 735–804)

Evening

God with me lying down,
God be with me rising up;
God with me in each ray of light,
Not a ray of joy without Him,
Not one without Him.
Christ with me sleeping,
Christ be with me waking,
Christ with me watching
Every day and night,
Each day and night.
God with me protecting,
Christ be with me directing,
The Spirit with me strengthening
Forever and evermore,
Forever and evermore.
Amen.

—*CARMINA GADELICA* (1900)

May 4

Morning

O Thou,
from whom to be turned is to fall,
to whom to be turned is to rise,
and in whom to stand is to abide forever;
grant me in all my duties Thy help,
in all my perplexities Thy guidance . . .
through Jesus Christ our Lord.
Amen.

—AUGUSTINE OF HIPPO (354–430)

Evening

Lord Jesus Christ, into Your hands
and into the hands of Your holy angels
I offer this night.
To You I entrust my soul and my body,
my father and my mother, my brothers and my sisters,
my friends and my neighbors, and all Christian people.
Keep us this night free from all sinful and wicked desires . . .
Enlighten our hearts with Your Holy Spirit,
that we may always obey Your commands.
And never separate us from the joy and comfort of Your love.
Amen.

—EDMUND OF ABINGDON (c. 1180–1240)

Morning

O God,
the source of eternal light,
You provide temporal light for the earth,
ruling over the sun and the moon
that all creatures may live and thrive.
The warmth and brightness of the sun
makes the flowers bloom and the crops grow. . . .
Guide me to find my rightful place in Your creation,
that in some small way
I may add to the beauty of Your handiwork.
And may Your eternal light
shine in the darkest corners of my soul,
that all shadow of sin may be expelled.
Amen.

—JACOB BOEHME (1575–1624)

Evening

O Lord our God,
if during this day I have sinned, whether in word or deed or thought,
forgive me all, for Thou art good and lovest mankind.
Grant me peaceful and undisturbed sleep,
and deliver me from all influence and temptation of the evil one.
Raise me up again in proper time that I may glorify Thee;
for Thou art blessed:
with Thine Only-begotten Son and Thine All-holy Spirit:
now and ever, and unto ages of ages.
Amen.

—EASTERN ORTHODOX PRAYER

MAY 6

Morning

O Lord Jesus Christ,
give us a measure of Thy Spirit
that we may be enabled to obey Thy teaching to pacify anger,
to take part in pity, to moderate desire,
to increase love, to put away sorrow,
to cast away vainglory,
not to be vindictive, not to fear death,
ever entrusting our spirit to immortal God,
who with Thee and the Holy Ghost liveth and reigneth
world without end.
Amen.

—APOLLONIUS OF ROME (2ND C.)

Evening

Thou has called us to Thyself, most merciful Father,
with love and with promises abundant . . .
We thank Thee for the privilege of prayer, and for Thine answers to prayer;
and we rejoice that Thou dost not answer according to our petitions.
We are blind, and are constantly seeking things which are not best for us.
If Thou didst grant all our desires according to our requests,
we should be ruined.
In dealing with our little children we give them,
not the things which they ask for,
but the things which we judge to be best for them; and Thou, our Father,
art by Thy providence overruling our ignorance and our headlong mistakes,
and art doing for us, not so much the things that we request of Thee
as the things that we should ask;
and we are, day by day, saved from peril and from ruin
by Thy better knowledge and by Thy careful love.
Amen.

—HENRY WARD BEECHER (1813–1887)

MAY 7

Morning

Let me do some deed for which Thou wilt remember me, Lord, for good,
and spare me according to the greatness of Thy mercy. . . .
Guard my going out and my coming in henceforth and for ever.
Prosper, I pray Thee, Thy servant this day,
and grant him mercy in the sight of those who meet him.
Amen.

—Lancelot Andrewes (1555–1626)

Evening

Blessed are You, O Lord,
the God of our fathers,
creator of the changes of day and night,
giving rest to the weary,
renewing the strength of those who are spent,
bestowing upon us occasions of song in the evening.
As You have protected us in the day that is past,
so be with us in the coming night;
keep us from every sin, every evil, and every fear;
for You are our light and salvation,
and the strength of our life.
To You be glory for endless ages.
Amen.

—Book of Common Prayer (1979)

Morning

Lord, help me today to realize that Thou wilt be speaking to me
through the events of the day,
through people, through things, and through all creation.
Give me ears, eyes and heart to perceive Thee,
however veiled Thy presence may be.
Give me insight to see through the exterior of things
to the interior truth.
Give me Thy Spirit of discernment.
O Lord, Thou knowest how busy I must be this day.
If I forget Thee, do not Thou forget me.
Amen.

—Sir Jacob Astley (1579–1652)

Evening

O my God,
I thank You for all the benefits which I have ever received from You,
and especially for the blessings of this day.
Give me light to see what sins I have committed today.
And grant me the grace to be truly sorry for them.
Amen.

—Anonymous Catholic prayer

May 9

Morning

Rise, beloved Christ, like a dove rising high in the sky,
its white feathers glistening in the sun.
Let us see Your purity of soul.
Like a sparrow keeping constant watch
over its nest of little ones,
watch over us day and night,
guarding us against all physical and spiritual dangers.
Like a turtledove hiding its offspring from all attackers,
hide us from the attacks of the devil.
Like a swallow, swooping down towards the earth,
swoop down upon us
and touch us with Your life-giving Spirit.
Amen.

—Bonaventure (1217–1274)

Evening

I give thanks that Your Son Jesus Christ,
who has shared our earthly life,
has now ascended to prepare our Heavenly life.
Grant that, through coming to know Him by faith on Earth,
I may come to know Him by sight in Heaven.
Amen.

—Gelasian Sacramentary (8th c.)

May 10

Morning

Give me a good digestion, Lord,
And also something to digest.
Give me a healthy body, Lord,
With sense to keep it at its best.
Give me a healthy mind, good Lord,
To keep the good and pure in sight,
Which seeing sin is not appalled,
But finds a way to set it right.
Give me a mind that is not bored,
That does not whimper, whine, or sigh.
Don't let me worry overmuch
About the fussy thing called "I."
Give me a sense of humor, Lord;
Give me the grace to see a joke,
To get some happiness from life
And pass it on to other folk.
Amen.

—Anonymous prayer found in Chester Cathedral

Evening

Lord, I sometimes wander away from You.
But this is not because I am deliberately turning my back on You.
It is because of the inconstancy of my mind.
I weaken in my intention to give my whole soul to You.
I fall back into thinking of myself as my own master.
But when I wander from You, my life becomes a burden,
and within me I find nothing but darkness . . .
So I come back to You, and confess that I have sinned against You.
And I know You will forgive me.
Amen.

—Aelred of Rievaulx (c. 1110–1167)

MAY 11

Almighty God, giver of all good gifts,
whose handiwork is lovely,
kindle in my life the true beauty of holiness,
so that graceful by obedience and fair by loving-kindness,
I may, through the ripening years,
show forth more and more the likeness of Thy dear Son Jesus Christ,
to whom with Thee and the Holy Ghost,
be all honor and glory, world without end.
Amen.

—*The Offices for Special Occasions* (1929)

Evening

To God be glory;
to the angels honor; to Satan confusion;
to the cross reverence; to the church exaltation;
to the departed quickening; to the penitent acceptance;
to the sick and infirm recovery and healing;
and to the four quarters of the world great peace and tranquility;
and on us who are weak and sinful
may the compassion and mercies of our God come and overshadow us.
Amen.

—Syrian Orthodox prayer for Vespers

Morning

O most sweet Jesus!
Turn Thy face towards me,
for this morning with all the power of my soul
I fly to Thee and salute Thee,
beseeching Thee that the
thousand times a thousand angels
who minister to Thee may praise Thee for me,
and that the thousand times ten thousand blessed spirits
who surround Thy throne may glorify Thee for me today.
May all that is beautiful and amiable in creatures
praise Thee for me,
and may all creation bless Thy holy name,
our consoling protection in time and in eternity.
Amen.

—HENRY SUSO (1295–1366)

Evening

Jesus, a look from You can embrace us with peaceful sleep,
and ensure that our dreams are pure and holy.
Sin shudders and falters at Your glance,
and guilt dissolves into tears of repentance.
Bring peace, Lord, to our weary minds,
and give rest to our tired limbs.
May we leave sin behind us,
and may our final reflections before sleep be prayers for Your mercy.
Amen.

—AMBROSE OF MILAN (c. 339–397)

Morning

Honor and praise be unto You, O Lord our God,
for all Your tender mercies. . . .
Continual thanks be unto You for creating us in Your own likeness;
for redeeming us by the precious blood of Your dear Son
when we were lost;
and for sanctifying us with the Holy Spirit. . . .
For all the benefits, O most merciful Father,
that we have received of Your goodness alone, we thank You;
and we beseech You to grant us always Your Holy Spirit,
that we may grow in grace, in steadfast faith,
and perseverance in all good works,
through Jesus Christ our Lord.
Amen.

—JOHN KNOX (1505–1572)

Evening

Lord, Thou knowest how I live,
What I've done amiss, forgive.
All of good I've tried to do
Strengthen, bless, and carry through.
All I love in safety keep,
Whilst in Thee I fall asleep.
Amen.

—HENRY VAN DYKE (1852–1933)

Morning

O fire of the Paraclete, . . .
from You the clouds issue and the air soars,
the rocks have their humors
and the waters bring forth their streams
and the earth sweats out green things growing.
And always You teach the learned,
those made happy by the inspiration of Wisdom.
So let there be praise to You
who are the sound of all praise
and the joy of life,
who are hope and powerful honor,
granting the gifts of light.
Amen.

—HILDEGARD OF BINGEN (1098–1179)

Evening

God the Father bless me,
Christ guard me,
the Holy Spirit enlighten me,
all the days of my life!
The Lord be the defender and guardian of my soul and my body,
now and always, world without end. . . .
The right hand of the Lord preserve me always to old age!
The grace of Christ perpetually defend me from the enemy!
Direct, Lord, my heart into the way of peace.
Lord God, deliver and help me.
Amen.

—BOOK OF CERNE (9TH C.)

May 15

Morning

Receive, Lord, all my liberty, my memory,
my understanding, and my whole will.
You have given me all that I have, all that I am,
and I surrender all to Your divine will, that You dispose of me.
Give me only Your love and Your grace.
With this I am rich enough, and I have no more to ask.
Amen.

—IGNATIUS OF LOYOLA (1491–1556)

Evening

Divine Lord,
Your night is so beautiful with its one large, bright star!
As I walk, this evening star seems to ride along
beside me through the sky.
Sometimes it feels that way with You too, Lord—
like You're not so much a leading Light
toward which my steps are wending,
as a faithful Friend keeping me company
as I walk through life.
Lord, lead, speak, intervene if it is Your will!
It would be easier if You would.
Just do not let me lose my way!
Still, perhaps I am already on the path You have selected.
Accompany me, then, if that is Your pleasure.
Be my Companion on the way.
And help me handle the obstacles
and lovely things I come across on this path
so my life may be a tribute to Your friendship.
Amen.

—JEANIE GUSHEE (1962–)

May 16

Morning

Lord God,
almighty and everlasting Father,
You have brought me in safety to this new day:
preserve me with Your mighty power,
that I may not fall into sin, nor be overcome by adversity;
and in all I do, direct me to the fulfilling of Your purpose,
through Jesus Christ our Lord.
Amen.

—Book of Common Prayer (1979)

Evening

Lord Jesus,
You are light from eternal lights.
You have dissolved all spiritual darkness
and my soul is filled with Your brightness.
Your light makes all things beautiful. . . .
You ordered night and day to follow each other peacefully. . . .
At night You give rest to our bodies. . . .
As I lay down on my bed at night,
may Your fingers draw down my eyelids.
Lay Your hand of blessing on my head
that righteous sleep may descend upon me.
Amen.

—Gregory of Nazianzus (c. 325–389)

Morning

O God our Father,
help me to a deeper trust in the life everlasting.
May I feel that this love which is now, ever shall be; . . .
this work of life is the work Thou hast given me to do,
and, when it is done, Thou wilt give me more;
this love, that makes all our life so glad,
flows from Thee, for Thou art love,
and we shall love forever.
Help me to feel how, day by day,
I see some dim shadow of the eternal day
that will break upon us at the last.
Amen.

—ROBERT COLLYER (1823–1912)

Evening

Into Thy hands, O Lord, I commend myself, my spirit, soul, and body:
Thou didst make, and didst redeem them . . .
And together with me,
all my friends and all that belongs to me.
Thou hast vouchsafed them to me, Lord, in Thy goodness. . . .
Let me remember Thee on my bed,
and search out my spirit;
let me wake up and be present with Thee;
I will lay me down in peace,
and take my rest:
for it is Thou, Lord, only, that makest me dwell in safety.
Amen.

—LANCELOT ANDREWES (1555–1626)

MAY 18

Morning

Lord,
how great a fire You can kindle from a tiny spark,
how great a tree You can grow from a tiny seed. . . .
My soul is so cold that by itself it has no joy,
yet You can light the fire of heavenly joy within me.
My soul is so feeble that by itself it has no faith;
yet by Your power my faith grows to a great height.
Thank You for prayer, for love, for joy, for faith;
let me always be prayerful, loving, joyful, and faithful.
Amen.

—GUIGO THE CARTHUSIAN (1140–1193)

Evening

Lord,
when I sleep let me not be made afraid,
but let my sleep be sweet,
that I may be enabled to serve Thee on the morrow.
Amen.

—ARCHBISHOP WILLIAM LAUD (1573–1645)

THE DESCENT OF THE HOLY SPIRIT

Morning

O Holy Ghost, O faithful Paraclete,
Love of the Father and the Son.
In whom Begetter and Begotten meet . . .
Bond that holdeth God to man,
Power that welds in one Humanity and Deity.
God making all that is before our day,
God guiding all that's made throughout our day,
Gift that abides through an eternity
Of giving, and is made no less.
Thy going forth preceded Time,
Thy pouring forth took place in Time.
The one, the well-spring of power and the river of grace,
The other, the flowing, the giving, the light on our face.
Thou camest forth from Thy transcendent day,
To make for us this shining feasting day.
Thou who alone art worthily adored
With Father and with Son.
To Thee in heart and word
Be honour, worship, grace,
Here and in every place,
World without end.
Amen.

—HILDEBERT OF LAVARDIN (1056–1133)

Evening

O Holy Spirit, the Spirit of Pentecost,
help me to clarify what is ambiguous,
to give warmth to what is indifferent,
to enlighten what is obscure,
and to be before the world a true and generous witness of Christ's love,
for no one can live without love.
Amen.

—POPE JOHN PAUL II (1920–2005)

ORDINARY TIME

There are two periods of time celebrated in the Western Christian church that are called "Ordinary Time." A fairly brief one follows shortly after Epiphany and lasts until Ash Wednesday, when the season of Lent is ushered in. The second, much longer Ordinary Time begins after Pentecost Sunday and lasts until it concludes with the Feast of Christ the King in late November. The following Sunday is the beginning of the season of Advent. All in all, the church spends about half of its time each year in Ordinary Time.

Ordinary Time takes its name from "ordinal" numbers, a way of counting the passage of different Sundays through the year. It was not intended to connote that these weeks of the church year are prosaic or uninteresting. Yet, just as a plain dark suit sets off the brilliance and color of a patterned tie, these stretches of Ordinary Time cause Lent and Advent to sparkle—Lent with somber magnificence and Advent with starlit wonder.

Morning

O God the Holy Spirit, most loving Comforter,
I pray that You will always turn what is evil in me into good
and what is good into what is better;
turn my mourning into joy, my wandering feet into the right path,
my ignorance into knowledge of Your truth,
my lukewarmness into zeal, my fear into love,
all my material good into a spiritual gift,
all my earthly desires into heavenly desires,
all that is transient into what lasts for ever,
everything human into what is divine,
everything created and finite
into that sovereign and immeasurable good,
which You Yourself are, O my God and Savior.
Amen.

—THOMAS À KEMPIS (1380–1471)

Evening

No, my Love, You are neither fire nor water
nor anything we could say of You.
You are what You are in Your glorious eternity.
You are: this is Your essence and Your name.
You are life, divine life, living life, unifying life.
You are all beatitude.
You are superadorable oneness, ineffable, incomprehensible.
In a word, You are Love, my Love.
Amen.

—MARIE OF THE INCARNATION (1599–1672)

Morning

Creator Spirit, by whose aid
The world's foundations first were laid,
Come, visit every pious mind;
Come, pour Thy joys on humankind;
From sin and sorrow set us free,
And make Thy temples worthy Thee.
O source of uncreated light,
The Father's promised Paraclete! . . .
Make us eternal truths receive,
And practise all that we believe:
Give us Thyself that we may see
The Father and the Son, by Thee.
Immortal honour, endless fame,
Attend the Almighty Father's name:
The Saviour Son be glorified,
Who for lost man's redemption died;
And equal adoration be,
Eternal Paraclete, to Thee.
Amen.

—RABANUS MAURUS (9TH C.); TRANSLATED BY JOHN DRYDEN (1631–1700)

Evening

Teach me, dear Lord, frequently and attentively to consider this truth:
that if I gain the whole world and lose You, in the end I have lost everything;
whereas if I lose the world and gain You,
in the end I have lost nothing.
Amen.

—CARDINAL JOHN HENRY NEWMAN (1801–1890)

MAY 22

Morning

Spirit of truth and love,
Life giving, holy Dove,
Speed forth Thy flight;
Move on the waters' face,
Spreading the beams of grace,
And in earth's darkest place
Let there be light!
Amen.

—JOHN MARRIOTT (1780–1825)

Evening

O Lord Jesus Christ,
who received the children who came to You,
receive also from me, Your child, this evening prayer.
Shelter me under the shadow of Your wings,
that in peace I may lie down and sleep;
and waken me in due time,
that I may glorify You,
for You alone are righteous and merciful.
Amen.

—ANONYMOUS

Morning

O God, we thank You for this earth, our home;
for the wide sky and the blessed sun,
for the salt sea and the running water,
for the everlasting hills and the never-resting winds,
for trees and the common grass underfoot.
We thank You for our senses by which we hear the song of birds,
and see the splendor of the summer fields,
and taste of the autumn fruits,
and rejoice in the feel of snow,
and smell the breath of the spring.
Grant us a heart wide open to all this beauty;
and save our souls from being so blind
that we pass unseeing when even the common thornbush
is aflame with Your glory,
O God our creator,
who lives and reigns for ever and ever.
Amen.

—WALTER RAUSCHENBUSCH (1861–1918)

Evening

O Jesus, You saw it all today.
You watched my every move.
You know my every thought.
How grateful I am
that You inspired my best,
and forgave my worst,
and—by Your grace—
will give me another chance tomorrow.
Amen.

—DAVID P. GUSHEE (1962–)

Morning

Who is this who smothers me with the most fragrant perfume?
Who is this who transforms my ugliness into perfect beauty?
Who is this who gives me the sweetest wine to drink,
and the finest food to eat?
It is You, Holy Spirit. You turn me into a bride fit for Jesus Christ.
You give me wine and food fit for a wedding in heaven.
My heart was weary, but now it is eager for love.
My soul was sad, but now it is full of joy.
Jesus gave His life for me. Now You, Holy Spirit, give me to Him.
Amen.

—Adam of St. Victor (12th c.)

Evening

Lord, I resolve by Thy Grace,
which I humbly beg
in the Name and for the sake
of the Lord Jesus,
that from this day forward,
I will resign myself and all relations
and secular concern,
to the entire management of Your good Providence.
Nor will I be anxious or solicitous
about events for the future,
in things relating only to this life.
Glory be to Thee, O Lord.
Amen.

—Susanna Wesley (1669–1742)

Morning

Grant to me, O Lord,
the royalty of inward happiness,
and the serenity . . . of joy,
and let the eternal Spirit of the Father
dwell in my soul and body,
filling every corner of my heart
with light and grace;
so that, bearing about with me
the infection of good courage,
I may be a diffuser of life . . .
Amen.

—ROBERT LOUIS STEVENSON (1850–1894)

Evening

I lie down this night with God,
and God will lie down with me;
I lie down this night with Christ,
and Christ will lie down with me.
I lie down this night with the Spirit,
and the Spirit will lie down with me.
God and Christ and the Spirit be lying down with me.
Amen.

—*CARMINA GADELICA* (1900)

Morning

God, I praise You:
Father all-powerful,
Christ, Lord and Savior,
Spirit of Love.
You reveal Yourself in the depths
of our being,
drawing us to share in Your life
and Your love.
One God, three Persons,
be near to us people
formed in Your image,
close to the world Your love
brings to life.
I ask this,
Father, Son, and Holy Spirit,
one God, true and living, for ever and ever.
Amen.

—ROMAN MISSAL FOR TRINITY SUNDAY

Evening

Almighty and everlasting God,
who hast given unto us Thy servants grace . . .
to acknowledge the glory of the eternal Trinity,
and . . . to worship the Unity;
I beseech Thee that Thou wouldst keep me steadfast in this faith,
and bring me at last to see Thee in Thy one and eternal glory,
O Father; who with the Son and the Holy Spirit livest and reignest,
One God, for ever and ever.
Amen.

—BOOK OF COMMON PRAYER (1928)

Morning

Bestow on me, O Lord,
a genial spirit and unwearied forbearance,
a mild, loving, patient heart,
kindly looks, pleasant, cordial speech and manner
that I may give offense to none,
but, as much as in me lies,
live in charity with all.
Amen.

—JOHANN ARNDT (c. 1555–1621)

Evening

O Lord, vouchsafe to look mercifully upon me,
and grant that I may ever choose the way of peace.
Amen.

—SARUM MISSAL (1085)

MAY 28

Morning

God, I want Thy guidance and direction in all I do.
Let Thy wisdom counsel me,
Thy hand lead me,
and Thine arm support me.
I put myself into Thy hands.
Breathe into my soul holy and heavenly desires.
Conform me to Thine own image.
Make me like my Saviour.
Enable me in some measure to live here on earth as He lived,
and to act in all things as He would have acted.
Amen.

—ASHTON OXENDEN (1808–1892)

Evening

Almighty God! . . .
To Thy goodness we commend ourselves this night
beseeching Thy protection of us through its darkness and dangers.
We are helpless and dependent; graciously preserve us.
For all whom we love and value, for every friend and connection,
we equally pray; however divided and far asunder,
we know that we are alike before Thee, and under Thine eye.
May we be equally united in Thy faith and fear,
in fervent devotion towards Thee,
and in Thy merciful protection this night.
Pardon oh Lord! the imperfections of these our prayers,
and accept them through the mediation of our blessed Savior.
Amen.

—JANE AUSTEN (1775–1817)

Morning

O Thou lover of mankind,
send down into my heart that
peace which the world cannot give,
and give me peace in this world.
O King of Peace, keep me in love and charity;
be my God, for I have none other beside Thee;
grant unto my soul the life of righteousness . . .
Amen.

—WALTER F. HOOK (1798–1875)

Evening

Heavenly Father, receive my evening sacrifice of praise,
and confession, and prayer, I beseech Thee.
I thank Thee for all the known and unknown mercies of another day,
for all the blessings of this life,
for all the means of grace, for all the riches of Thy salvation,
and for the hope of glory, that blessed hope,
the coming of our Lord Jesus Christ and
our gathering together unto Him.
We are one day nearer to that day.
Teach us to live every day as those whose citizenship is in heaven.
Amen.

—HANDLEY CARR GLYN MOULE (1841–1920)

Morning

I pray You, O most gentle Jesus, . . .
deliver me from all evils, . . .
give me lively faith,
a firm hope
and perfect charity,
so that I may love You with all my heart,
and all my soul
and all my strength.
Make me firm and steadfast in good works,
and grant me perseverance in Your service
so that I may be able to please You always.
Amen.

—CLARE OF ASSISI (1194–1253)

Evening

Thanks be to Thee, holy Father,
for Thy Sacred Name which Thou hast caused to dwell in our hearts.
Thou, O Lord, has created all things for Thine own Name's sake;
to all men Thou hast given meat and drink to enjoy,
that they might give thanks to Thee,
but to us Thou has graciously given spiritual meat and drink,
together with life eternal, through Thy Servant.
Be mindful of Thy church, O Lord;
deliver it from all evil, perfect it in Thy love, sanctify it,
and gather it from the four winds
into the kingdom which Thou hast prepared for it.
Let Jesus, His Grace, draw near, and let this world pass away.
Amen.

—THE DIDACHE (1ST C.)

May 31

Morning

O heavenly Father,
the author and fountain of all truth,
the bottomless sea of all understanding,
send, I beseech Thee, Thy Holy Spirit
into my heart,
and lighten my understanding
with the beams of Thy heavenly grace.
I ask this, O merciful Father,
for Thy dear Son, our Saviour, Jesus Christ's sake.
Amen.

—Nicholas Ridley (1500–1555)

Evening

Fountain of Light, Source of Light, hear my prayer.
Drive away from me the shadow of sin.
Seek me, kindly Light.
You, who created us in holiness, who condemned our sin,
who redeemed us from our sin, sustain me by Your power.
The labour of the day is over, and now I rest safely at home.
Make this home Your home, and protect me with Your grace.
The sun has fallen below the earth, and now the darkness is here.
Let Your uncreated light shine upon my dark and weary soul.
Pour Your gentle light into my dull mind,
filling my head with holy thoughts.
Pour Your glorious light into my cold breast,
kindling holy love within my heart.
From horror, lust and fear, guard me while I sleep.
And if I cannot sleep, let my eyes behold Your heavenly host.
Amen.

—Alcuin of York (c. 735–804)

JUNE 1

Morning

O holy Jesus, meek Lamb of God;
Bread that came down from heaven;
light and life of all holy souls:
help me to a true and living faith in You.
Open Yourself within me with all Your holy nature and spirit,
that I may be born again by You,
and in You be a new creation,
brought alive and revived,
led and ruled by Your Holy Spirit.
Amen.

—WILLIAM LAW (1686–1761)

Evening

Eternal God, the refuge of all Your children,
in our weakness You are our strength,
in our darkness our light,
in our sorrow our comfort and peace.
May I always live in Your presence,
and serve You in my daily life;
through Jesus Christ our Lord.
Amen.

—BONIFACE (c. 680–754)

JUNE 2

Morning

I render unto Thee my thanksgiving, O Lord my God,
Father of our Lord and Saviour Jesus Christ,
by all means, at all times, in all places;
for that Thou hast sheltered, assisted, supported,
and led me on through the time past of my life
and brought me to this hour.
And I pray and beseech Thee,
O God and loving Lord,
grant me to pass this day . . .
without sin,
with all joy,
health and salvation.
Amen.

—LITURGY OF ST. MARK (2ND c.)

Evening

I praise Your magnificent goodness at close of day,
and especially the ways You have blessed me
during its hours. I have enjoyed a home and food,
and there are people who love me.
There are also those whom I love,
to whom it is my joy and responsibility to act with grace,
and for this I thank You.
I believe You give each of Your children
a mission, a way to bless the world.
For those who are lonely, who are still searching
for their way to love in the world,
I pray that You will make it very clear to them.
As for me, in this smooth, soft place
of Your kindly care,
I lift up my heart and bless Your name.
Amen.

—JEANIE GUSHEE (1962–)

Morning

May I live in the peace that comes from You.
May I journey towards Your city,
sailing through the waters of sin untouched by the waves,
borne serenely along by the Holy Spirit.
Night and day may I give You praise and thanks,
because You have shown me that
all things belong to You,
and all blessings are gifts from You.
To You, the essence of wisdom,
the foundation of truth,
be glory for evermore.
Amen.

—Clement of Alexandria (c. 150–c. 220)

Evening

The day is Yours, O God, and the night also.
In the morning, You renew my strength;
in the evening, I find the shelter of Your wing.
You are my Sun, and apart from You my toil is weary and blind,
and there is no glory in my joy.
You are my Shade; for in You my restless soul finds rest.
Abiding God, enter fully into my life.
Amen.

—James Martineau (1805–1900)

JUNE 4

Lord, You are like a wildflower.
You spring up in places where we least expect You.
The bright colour of Your grace dazzles us.
When we reach down to pluck You, hoping to possess You for our own,
You blow away in the wind.
And if we tried to destroy You, by stamping on You and kicking You,
You would come back to life.
Lord, may we come to expect You anywhere and everywhere.
May we rejoice in Your beauty.
Far from trying to possess You, may You possess us.
And may You forgive us for all the times
when we have sinned against You.
Amen.

—HENRY SUSO (1295–1366)

Evening

O Heavenly Comforter, Spirit of truth,
present in all places and filling all things;
Treasury of blessings and Giver of life:
come and dwell in us, cleanse us from every impurity,
and of Your goodness, save our souls.
Amen.

—ROMANIAN ORTHODOX PRAYER

JUNE 5

Morning

Lord, I believe in You: increase my faith.
I trust in You: strengthen my trust.
I love You: let me love You more and more.
I am sorry for my sins: deepen my sorrow.
I worship You as my first beginning,
I long for You as my last end;
I praise You as my constant helper,
and call on You as my loving protector.
Guide me by Your wisdom,
correct me with Your justice,
comfort me with Your mercy,
protect me with Your power.
Amen.

—POPE CLEMENT XI (1699–1721)

Evening

My Jesus, I love Thee, I know Thou art mine;
For Thee all the follies of sin I resign.
My gracious Redeemer, my Savior art Thou;
If ever I loved Thee my Jesus 'tis now.
I love Thee because Thou hast first loved me,
And purchased my pardon on Calvary's tree. . . .
I'll love Thee in life, I will love Thee in death,
And praise Thee as long as Thou lendest me breath.
Amen.

—WILLIAM R. FEATHERSTON (1846–1873)

JUNE 6

Morning

Lord God, open my heart and illuminate it
with the grace of Your Holy Spirit.
By this grace may I always seek to do
what is pleasing to You;
direct my thoughts and feelings so that I at last
come to the unending joys of heaven.
Thus on earth may I keep Your commandments,
and so be worthy of Your everlasting reward.
Amen.

—The Venerable Bede (675–735)

Evening

O Lord, whose way is perfect,
help me, I pray, always to trust in Your goodness,
that walking with You
and following You in all simplicity,
I may possess a quiet and contented mind
and cast all my care on You,
who care for me . . .
for Your dear Son's sake, Jesus Christ.
Amen.

—Christina Rossetti (1830–1894)

June 7

Morning

Jesus, receive my heart,
and bring me to Thy love.
All my desire Thou art.
Kindle fire within me,
that I may win to Thy love,
and see Thy face in bliss
which shall never cease,
in heaven with never an ending.
Amen.

—Richard Rolle (1295–1349)

Evening

Lord,
Keep me safe this night,
Secure from all my fears;
May angels guard me while I sleep,
Till morning light appears.
Amen.

—John Leland (1754–1841)

June 8

Morning

Blessing and honor and thanksgiving and praise,
more than I can utter,
more than I can conceive,
be unto Thee, O holy and glorious Trinity,
Father, Son, and Holy Ghost,
by all angels,
by all men,
all creatures,
for ever and ever.
Amen.

—Bishop Thomas Ken (1637–1711)

Evening

Spirit of truth,
You are the reward to the saints,
the comforter of souls,
light in the darkness,
riches to the poor,
treasure to lovers,
food for the hungry,
comfort for the wanderer;
to sum up,
You are the one in whom all treasures are contained.
Amen.

—Mary Magdalen dei Pazzi (1566–1607)

June 9

Morning

May none of God's wonderful works
keep silence, night or morning!
Bright stars, high mountains, the depths of the seas,
sources of rushing rivers:
may all these break into song as we sing
to Father, Son and Holy Spirit.
May all the angels in the heavens reply:
Amen! Amen! Amen!
Power, praise, honor, and eternal glory
to God, the only giver of grace!
Amen! Amen! Amen!

—Prayer from Egypt (3rd c.)

Evening

Ah, Lord, to whom all hearts are open,
You can pilot the ship of my soul far better than I can . . .
Do not let me be carried hither and thither by wandering thoughts,
but, forgetting all else, let me see and hear You alone.
Renew my spirit; kindle in me Your light, that it may shine within me,
and my heart may burn in love and adoration for You.
Let Your Holy Spirit dwell in me continually,
and make me Your temple and sanctuary.
Fill me with divine love and light and life,
with devout and heavenly thoughts,
with comfort and strength, with joy and peace.
Amen.

—Johann Arndt (c. 1555–1621)

Morning

O Lord,
take my mind and think through it;
take my lips and speak through them;
take my life and live out Your life;
take my heart and set it on fire with love for Thee;
and guide me ever by Thy Holy Spirit,
through Jesus Christ our Lord.
Amen.

—WILLIAM H. M. H. AITKEN (1841–1927)

Evening

May You be blessed forever, Lord,
for not abandoning me when I abandoned You.
May You be blessed forever, Lord,
for offering Your hand of love in my darkest, most lonely moment.
May You be blessed forever, Lord,
for putting up with such a stubborn soul as mine.
May You be blessed forever, Lord,
for loving me more than I love myself.
May You be blessed forever, Lord,
for continuing to pour out Your blessings upon me,
even though I respond so poorly.
May You be blessed forever, Lord,
for drawing out the goodness in all people, even including me.
May You be blessed forever, Lord,
for repaying our sin with Your love.
May You be blessed forever, Lord,
for being constant and unchanging, amidst all the changes of the world.
May You be blessed forever, Lord,
for Your countless blessings on me and on all Your creatures.
Amen.

—TERESA OF ÁVILA (1515–1582)

JUNE 11

Morning

Jesus, our mighty Lord,
Our strength in sadness,
The Father's conquering Word,
True source of gladness;
Your Name I glorify,
O Jesus, throned on high;
You gave Yourself to die
For our salvation.
Good Shepherd of Your sheep,
Your own defending,
In love Your children keep
To life unending.
You are Yourself the Way:
Lead us then day by day
In Your own steps, we pray,
O Lord most holy.
Amen.

—CLEMENT OF ALEXANDRIA (c. 150–c. 220)

Evening

May the God of peace bless this house.
Deep peace of the running waves to us.
Deep peace of the flowing air to us.
Deep peace of the quiet earth to us.
Deep peace of the shining stars to us.
Deep peace of the shades of night to us,
moon and stars always give light to us.
May we sleep in the peace of Christ.
Amen.

—GAELIC NIGHTTIME BLESSING

June 12

Morning

For flowers that bloom about our feet,
For tender grass so fresh, so sweet,
For the song of bird and hum of bee,
For all things fair we hear or see;
Father in heaven, we thank Thee!

. . .

For each new morning with its light,
For rest and shelter of the night,
For health and food, for love and friends,
For everything Thy goodness sends,
Father in heaven, we thank Thee.
Amen.

> —Ralph Waldo Emerson (1802–1882)

Evening

My God, I believe most firmly that You watch over all who hope in You,
and that we can want for nothing when we rely upon You in all things.
Therefore I am resolved for the future . . .
to cast all my cares upon You. . . .
Let others seek happiness in their wealth and in their talents. . . .
as for me, my Rock and my Refuge,
my confidence in You fills me with hope.
For You, my Divine Protector, alone have settled me in hope.
"This confidence can never be vain.
No one, who has hoped in God,
has ever been confounded."
I am assured, therefore, of my eternal happiness,
for I firmly hope in it and all my hope is in You.
Amen.

> —Claude La Colombière (1641–1682)

June 13

Morning

O Father, light up the small duties of this day;
may they shine with the beauty of Your face.
May I believe that glory can dwell
in the commonest task every day.
Amen.

—Augustine of Hippo (354–430)

Evening

O Lord; O King, resplendent on the citadel of heaven,
all hail continually;
and of Your clemency upon Your people have mercy.
Lord, whom the hosts of cherubim in songs and hymns
with praise continually proclaim, upon us eternally have mercy . . .
O Christ, hymned by Your one and only church
throughout the world,
to whom the sun, and moon, and stars, the land and sea,
ever do service, have mercy . . .
O King of kings, blessed redeemer;
upon those who have been ransomed from the power of death,
by Your own blood, have mercy . . .
O sun of righteousness, in all unclouded glory,
supreme dispenser of justice,
in that great day when You strictly judge all nations . . .
in Your pity, Lord, then have mercy on us.
Amen.

—Dunstan (c. 908–988)

June 14

Morning

Eternal goodness,
You want me to gaze into You
and see that You love me,
to see that You love me gratuitously
so that I may love everyone
with the very same love.
You want me, then,
to love and serve my neighbors gratuitously,
by helping them
spiritually and materially
as much as I can. . . .
God, come to my assistance!
Amen.

—CATHERINE OF SIENA (1347–1380)

Evening

Our Father in heaven,
hallowed be Your name.
Your kingdom come.
Your will be done
on earth as it is in heaven.
Give us this day our daily bread.
And forgive us our debts,
as we forgive our debtors.
And do not lead us into temptation,
but deliver us from the evil one.
For Yours is the kingdom and the power and the glory forever.
Amen.

—JESUS CHRIST (MATTHEW 6:9–13)

JUNE 15

Morning

Eternal King without beginning,
You who are before all worlds,
my Maker who hast summoned all things
from non-being into this life:
bless this day that You, in Your inscrutable goodness,
give to me. By the power of Your blessing
enable me at all times in this coming day
to speak and act for You, to Your glory,
in Your fear, according to Your will,
with a pure spirit,
with humility, patience, love,
with gentleness, peace, courage,
wisdom and prayer,
aware everywhere of Your presence . . .
Amen.

—ELDER SOPHRONY OF ESSEX (1896–1993)

Evening

God,
to whom all hearts are open,
to whom all wills speak
and from whom no secret is hidden,
I beg You,
so to cleanse the intent of my heart
with the unutterable gift of Your grace,
that I may perfectly love You
and worthily praise You.
Amen.

—*THE CLOUD OF UNKNOWING* (14TH C.)

JUNE 16

Morning

Bless me, and all I am to go about and do this day,
with the blessing of Thy love and mercy.
Continue Thy grace and love in Jesus Christ upon me,
and give me a mind cheerfully to follow Thy leadings
and execute Thine appointment.
Let Thy Holy Spirit guide me
in my beginning,
and my progress,
on to my last end.
Amen.

—Jacob Boehme (1575–1624)

Evening

Abide with me, O good Lord,
through the night,
guarding, keeping, guiding, sustaining, sanctifying,
and with Thy love gladdening me,
that in Thee I may ever live . . .
through Jesus Christ our Lord.
Amen.

—Edward White Benson (1829–1896)

Morning

Almighty and everlasting God,
be Thou present with me in all my duties,
and grant the protection of Thy presence
to all that dwell in this house,
that Thou mayest be known
to be the Defender of this household,
and the Inhabitant of this dwelling.
Amen.

—GELASIAN SACRAMENTARY (8TH C.)

Evening

Jesus, You are my true friend . . .
You take a part in all my misfortunes;
You take them on Yourself;
You know how to change them into blessings.
You listen to me with the greatest kindness
when I relate my troubles to You,
and You always have balm to pour on my wounds.
I find You at all times, I find You everywhere, You never go away;
if I have to change my dwelling, I find You wherever I go.
You are never weary of listening to me,
You are never tired of doing me good.
I am certain of being beloved by You if I love You;
my goods are nothing to You,
and by bestowing Yours on me You never grow poor.
However miserable I may be,
no one nobler or wiser or even holier can come between You and me,
and deprive me of Your friendship;
and death, which tears us away from all other friends,
will unite me forever to You. . . .
Amen.

—CLAUDE LA COLOMBIÈRE (1641–1682)

June 18

O burning mountain, O chosen sun,
O perfect moon, O fathomless well,
O unattainable height,
O clearness beyond measure,
O wisdom without end,
O mercy without limit,
O strength beyond resistance,
O crown of all majesty,
the humblest You created sings Your praise.
Amen.

—MECHTHILD OF MAGDEBURG (c. 1207–c. 1290)

Evening

Day is done,
Gone the sun
From the lake, from the hills, from the sky.
Safely rest;
All is blest!
All is well.
God is nigh.
Amen.

—ANONYMOUS; LYRICS OF "TAPS," MILITARY/SCOUTING SONG (19TH C.)

June 19

Morning

O God, our Father,
direct and control me in every part of my life;
my tongue, that I speak no false, angry, or impure words;
my actions, that I do nothing to shame myself or hurt others.
Control my mind that I may think no evil, bitter, or irreverent thoughts.
Control my heart, that it be set only on pleasing You;
through my Lord Jesus Christ.
Amen.

—Catholic prayer

Evening

Jesus, how sweet is the very thought of You!
You fill my heart with joy.
The sweetness of Your love surpasses the sweetness of honey.
Nothing sweeter than You can be described;
no words can express the joy of Your love.
Only those who have tasted Your love for themselves can comprehend it.
In Your love You listen to all my prayers,
even when my wishes are childish, my words confused,
and my thoughts foolish.
And you answer my prayers, not according to
my own misdirected desires,
which would bring only bitter misery;
but according to my real needs,
which brings me sweet joy.
Thank You, Jesus, for giving Yourself to me.
Amen.

—Bernard of Clairvaux (1090–1153)

June 20

Morning

O God,
I bless You that You have permitted me to lie down in sleep,
and to awake this morning in safety.
You have dispersed the darkness of another night;
may no shadow of my sin obscure the sunshine of
Your favor and love . . .
Direct, control, suggest this day all my designs
and thoughts and actions, that every power of my body,
and every faculty of my mind,
may unite in devotedness to Your sole service and glory.
And all I ask for Jesus' sake.
Amen.

—JOHN MACDUFF (1818–1895)

Evening

My God, I am Yours for time and eternity.
Teach me to cast myself entirely into the arms of Your loving Providence
with the most lively, unlimited confidence
in Your compassionate, tender pity. . . .
Take from my heart all painful anxiety;
suffer nothing to sadden me but sin,
nothing to delight me but the hope of coming to the possession of You,
my God and my all,
in Your everlasting Kingdom.
Amen.

—CATHERINE MCAULEY (1778–1841)

June 21

Morning

Father, I thank Thee for the night,
And for the pleasant morning light,
For rest, and food, and loving care,
And all that makes the world so fair.
Help me to do the things I should,
To be to others kind and good,
In all I do, in work and play,
To grow more loving every day.
Amen.

—Rebecca J. Weston (1835–1895)

Evening

Into Thy hands, most blessed Jesus,
I commend my soul and body,
for Thou hast redeemed both by Thy most precious blood.
So bless and sanctify my sleep to me,
that it may be temperate, holy, and safe,
a refreshment to my weary body,
to enable it so to serve my soul,
that both may serve Thee with never-failing duty.
Visit, I beseech Thee, O Lord,
this habitation with Thy mercy,
and me with Thy grace and favour. . . .
Amen.

—Jeremy Taylor (1613–1667)

JUNE 22

Morning

Show me Your ways, O Lord;
Teach me Your paths.
Lead me in Your truth and teach me,
For You are the God of my salvation;
On You I wait all the day.
Amen.

—Psalm 25:4–5

Evening

I am bending my knee
In the eye of the Father who created me,
In the eye of the Son who purchased me,
In the eye of the Spirit who cleansed me,
In friendship and affection.
Through Thine Own Anointed One, O God,
Bestow upon us fullness in our need,
Love towards God,
The affection of God,
The smile of God,
The wisdom of God,
The grace of God,
The fear of God,
And the will of God
To do in the world of the Three,
As angels and saints
Do in heaven;
Each shade and light,
Each day and night,
Each time in kindness,
Give Thou as Thy Spirit.
Amen.

—Ann Macdonald (19th c.)

Morning

My Heavenly Father,
I thank You, through Jesus Christ Your beloved Son,
that You kept me safe from all evil and danger last night.
I ask You to save me today as well from every evil and sin,
so that all I do and the way that I live will please You.
I put myself in Your care, body and soul, and all that I have.
Let Your holy angels be with me,
so that the evil enemy will not gain power over me.
Amen.

—Martin Luther (1483–1546)

Evening

I thank You, O God, through Your Child, Jesus Christ our Lord,
because You have enlightened us
and revealed to us the light that is incorruptible.
The day's allotted span is over;
we have reached the beginning of the night.
We have had our fill of that daylight which You created for our pleasure.
And now that evening has come and again we have no lack of light,
we praise Your holiness and glory,
through Your only Son, our Lord Jesus Christ.
Through Him the glory and power that are His
and the honor that is the Holy Spirit's
are also Yours, as they will be throughout
the unending succession of ages.
Amen.

—Hippolytus of Rome (c. 190–c. 236)

Morning

Heavenly Father,
I most heartily thank Thee,
that it has pleased Thy fatherly goodness
to take care of me this night past.
I most entirely beseech Thee, most merciful Father,
to show the same kindness toward me this day,
in preserving my body and soul;
that I may neither think, breathe, speak, nor do anything
that may be displeasing to Thy fatherly goodness,
dangerous to myself, or hurtful to my neighbor;
but that all my doings may be agreeable to Your most blessed will,
which is always good;
that they may advance Thy glory, answer to my vocation,
and profit my neighbor,
whom I ought to love as myself;
that, whenever Thou callest me hence,
I may be found the child not of darkness but of light;
through Jesus Christ our Lord.
Amen.

—THOMAS BECON (c. 1512–1567)

Evening

I thank Thee, O Lord and Master,
for teaching me how to pray simply and sincerely to Thee,
and for hearing me when I so call upon Thee.
I thank Thee for saving me from my sins and sorrows,
and for directing all my ways this day.
Lead me ever onwards to Thyself;
for the sake of Jesus Christ,
my Lord and Saviour.
Amen.

—JOHN SERGIEFF (1829–1908)

June 25

Morning

All glory and thanks, all honour and power, all love and obedience,
be to the blessed and undivided Trinity, one God Eternal.
The heavens declare Thy glory,
the earth confesses Thy providence,
the sea manifests Thy power,
and every spirit, and every understanding creature
celebrates Thy greatness for ever and ever.
All glory and majesty, all praises and dominion be unto Thee, O God,
Father, Son, and Holy Ghost, for ever and ever.
Amen.

—Jeremy Taylor (1613–1667)

Evening

May the Light of Lights come
To my dark heart from Thy place;
May the Spirit's wisdom come
To my heart's tablet from my Savior.
Be the peace of the Spirit mine this night,
Be the peace of the Son mine this night,
Be the peace of the Father mine this night.
The peace of all peace be mine this night,
Each morning and evening of my life.
Amen.

—Celtic prayer

June 26

Morning

O God, I thank Thee for all the joy I have had in life.
Amen.

—Byrhtnoth (c. 931–991)

Evening

Slowly we are turning once again
to look into the dark, star-sprinkled space
through which our planet is traveling.
All life is aware of the approaching view,
and the sunset beauty of this day's end
is an overture to the awesome grandeur
of the eternal vision that awaits us.
As the Earth turns outward,
may my thoughts turn inward
to the Sacred Mystery that dwells in my heart.
At the end of this day
I sing a song of thanksgiving
for the wonder of life.
I lift up my voice in gratitude
for all this day has held for me
as I turn my memory to its flood of gifts.
Blessed are You, Divine Mystery,
who has chosen to dwell within me
and has ended this day
with zestful life, beauty, love,
and the discipline of my trials and temptations.
Blessed are You, O God.
Most blessed are You.
Amen.

—Joyce Rupp (1943–)

June 27

Morning

O Good Jesu,
Word of the Father,
the brightness of the Father's glory,
whom angels desire to behold;
teach us to do Your will;
that guided by Your good Spirit,
we may come to that blessed city where there is everlasting day.
Amen.

—Gregory the Great (540–604)

Evening

The night is here.
Be near to me, dear Jesus.
Be a bright candle shining in the dark,
driving the sin from my heart. . . .
The moon casts her gentle rays.
Guide me, dear Jesus.
Guide my steps through this gloomy path
that I may arrive safely in heaven.
The stars glisten in the sky.
Teach me, dear Jesus,
Teach me to discern the truth amidst falsehood,
that even now I may see signs of Your glory.
Amen.

—Johann Freylinghausen (1670–1739)

June 28

Morning

Thou Great First Cause, least understood,
Who all my sense confined
To know but this, that Thou art good,
And that myself am blind! . . .
Save me alike from foolish pride,
Or impious discontent,
At aught Thy wisdom has denied,
Or aught Thy goodness lent.
Teach me to feel another's woe,
To hide the fault I see;
That mercy I to others show,
That mercy show to me.
Mean though I am, not wholly so,
Since quickened by Thy breath;
O lead me wheresoe'er I go
Through this day's life or death.
This day be bread and peace my lot:
All else beneath the sun
Thou knowest if best bestowed or not,
And let Thy will be done. . . .
Amen.

—Alexander Pope (1688–1744)

Evening

The day Thou gavest, Lord, is ended;
The darkness falls at Thy behest.
To Thee my morning prayers ascended;
Thy praise shall hallow now my rest.
Amen.

—John Ellerton (1826–1893)

JUNE 29

Morning

O Lord our heavenly Father, Almighty and everlasting God,
who hast safely brought us to the beginning of this day;
defend us in the same with Thy mighty power,
and grant that this day we fall into no sin,
neither run into any kind of danger;
but that all our doings may be ordered by Thy governance,
to do always what is righteous in Thy sight; through Jesus Christ our Lord.
Amen.

—BOOK OF COMMON PRAYER (1662)

Evening

I love You, O my God,
and my only desire is to love You until the last breath of my life.
I love You, and I would rather die loving You
than live without loving You.
I love You, Lord, and the only grace I ask is to love You eternally.
My God, if my tongue cannot say in every moment that I love You,
I want my heart to repeat it to You as often as I draw breath.
Amen.

—JEAN-BAPTISTE VIANNEY, CURÉ D'ARS (1786–1859)

JUNE 30

Morning

Grant me, O Lord Christ,
to desire to have Thee as my Savior,
not in the next world, but in this;
that Thou wilt change and alter
all that is within me,
as Thou didst help the blind to see and the lame to walk;
that Thy temper may be formed and begotten in my heart,
Thy humility and self-denial,
Thy love to the Father,
the desire of doing His will and seeking only His honor;
that so the kingdom of God may be in me now,
and my possession forever,
world without end.
Amen.

—WILLIAM LAW (1686–1761)

Evening

I lie down tonight. . . . with God,
and God will lie down with me.
I will not lie down with Satan,
nor shall Satan lie down with me.
O God of the poor, help me this night;
omit me not entirely from Thy treasure-house.
For the many wounds that I inflicted on Thee,
I cannot this night enumerate them. . . .
Do not forget me in Thy dwelling place;
do not exact from me for my transgressions.
Do not omit me in Thine ingathering,
in Thine ingathering.
Amen.

—GAELIC PRAYER OF SCOTLAND (14TH C.)

July 1

Morning

If I have faltered more or less
In my great task of happiness;
If I have moved among my race
And shown no glorious morning face;
If beams from happy human eyes
Have moved me not; if morning skies,
Books, and my food, and summer rain
Knocked on my sullen heart in vain:
Lord, Thy most pointed pleasure take
And stab my spirit broad awake! . . .
Amen.

—Robert Louis Stevenson (1850–1894)

Evening

O God,
Thou art the life of all who live,
the light of the faithful,
the strength of all who labor,
and the repose of those who sleep in Christ.
I thank Thee for the timely blessings of the day,
and humbly beseech Thy merciful protection all the night.
Bring me, I pray Thee,
in safety to the morning hours,
when I shall praise Thee again;
through Him who died for us and rose again.
Amen.

—Book of Common Prayer (1928)

July 2

Morning

Glory to You, O Lord,
for the feast-day of life!
Glory to You for the perfumes of lilies and roses.
Glory to You for each different taste of berries and fruit.
Glory to You for the sparkling silver look of early-morning dew,
Glory to You for the joy of dawn's awakening.
Glory to You for eternal life, and the kingdom of heaven,
Glory to You, O God, from age to age.
Amen.

—Metropolitan Tryphon (1861–1934)

Evening

O Thou transcendent,
Nameless, the fiber and the breath,
Light of the light, shedding forth universes, Thou center of them,
Thou mightier center of the true, the good, and the loving,
Thou moral, spiritual foundation—affection's source—Thou reservoir,
(O pensive soul of me—O thirst unsatisfied—waitest not there?
Waitest not haply for us somewhere there the Comrade perfect?)
Thou pulse—Thou motive of the stars, suns, systems,
That, circling, move in order, safe, harmonious,
Athwart the shapeless vastness of space,
How should I think, how breathe a single breath,
how speak if out of myself,
I could not launch, to those superior universes?
Amen.

—Walt Whitman (1819–1892)

Morning

Work Thy holy will in me and through me this day.
Protect me, guide me, bless me, within and without,
that I may do something this day for love of Thee;
something which shall please Thee;
and that I may, this evening, be nearer to Thee. . . .
Lead me, O Lord, in a straight way unto Thyself,
and keep me in Thy grace unto the end.
Amen.

—Edward Bouverie Pusey (1800–1882)

Evening

O eternal God, King of all creation,
who hast brought me to this hour,
forgive me the sins which I have committed this day
in thought, word, and deed,
and cleanse, O Lord, my humble soul
from every stain of flesh and spirit.
Grant me, O Lord, to pass through the sleep of this night in peace,
to rise from my lowly bed,
to please Thy holy name all the days of my life . . .
Amen.

—Macarius of Egypt (c. 300–390)

July 4

Morning

Most gracious Lord God,
from whom proceedeth every good and perfect gift,
I offer to Thy divine majesty my unfeigned praise and thanksgiving
for all Thy mercies toward me. . . .
Instruct me in the particulars of my duty,
and suffer me not to be tempted above what Thou givest me strength to bear.
Take care, I pray Thee, of my affairs
and more and more direct me in Thy truth . . .
Suffer me not to be drawn from Thee by the blandishments of the world. . . .
Render me charitable, pure, holy, patient and heavenly minded. . . .
Bless, O Lord, the whole race of mankind. . . .
Bless my friends, and grant me grace to forgive my enemies
as heartily as I desire forgiveness of Thee, my heavenly Father.
I beseech Thee to defend me . . . and do more for me
than I can think or ask,
for Jesus Christ's sake, in whose most holy name I pray.
Amen.

—George Washington (1732–1799)

Evening

We bless Thee for the inspired souls of all ages
who saw afar the shining city of God,
and by faith left the profit of the present to follow their vision. . . .
Make us determined to live by truth and not by lies,
to found our common life on the eternal foundations
of righteousness and love. . . .
Help us to make the welfare of all the supreme law of our land,
so that our commonwealth may be built strong and secure
on the love of all its citizens.
Cast down the throne of Mammon who ever grinds the life of men,
and set up Thy throne, O Christ, for Thou didst die that men might live. . . .
Our Master, once more we make Thy faith our prayer: Thy Kingdom come!
Amen.

—Walter Rauschenbusch (1861–1918)

July 5

Keep us, O God, from all pettiness,
let us be large in thought, in word, in deed.
Let us be done with the fault finding, and leave off all self-seeking.
May we put away all pretense, and meet each other face to face
without self-pity and without prejudice.
May we never be hasty in judgment and always generous.
Let us take time for all things, and make us to grow
calm, serene, and gentle.
Teach us to put into action our better impulses,
straightforward and unafraid.
Grant that we may realize that it is the little things of life
that create differences,
that in the big things of life, we are as one.
And, O Lord God, let us not forget to be kind!
Amen.

—MARY STUART, QUEEN OF SCOTLAND (1542–1587)

Evening

May the grace of the Lord Jesus sanctify us and keep us from all evil;
may He drive far from us all hurtful things,
and purify both our souls and bodies;
may He bind us to Himself by the bond of love,
and may His peace abound in our hearts.
Amen.

—GREGORIAN SACRAMENTARY (8TH C.)

Morning

O Lord God,
grant us always,
whatever the world may say,
to content ourselves with what You say,
and to care only for Your approval,
which will outweigh all worlds;
for Jesus Christ's sake.
Amen.

—CHARLES GORDON (1833–1885)

Evening

I thank Thee, my Heavenly Father,
through Jesus Christ, Thy dear Son,
that Thou hast graciously kept me this day;
and I pray Thee that Thou wouldst forgive me
all my sins where I have done wrong,
and graciously keep me this night.
For into Thy hands I commend myself,
my body and soul, and all things.
Let Thy holy angel be with me,
that the wicked foe may have no power over me.
Amen.

—MARTIN LUTHER (1483–1546)

July 7

Morning

O Lord my God,
who hast chased the slumber from my eyes,
and once more brought me here to lift up my hands
unto Thee and to praise Thy just judgments,
accept my prayer and supplication, and
give me faith and love.
Amen.

—Greek Liturgy (3rd c.)

Evening

Almighty and eternal God,
the Disposer of all the affairs of the world,
there is not one circumstance
so great as not to be subject to Thy power,
nor so small but it comes within Thy care.
Amen.

—Queen Anne of Great Britain and Ireland (1665–1714)

July 8

Morning

Let me, with a gladsome mind
Praise the Lord, for He is kind;
For His mercies shall endure,
Ever faithful, ever sure.
Amen.

—John Milton (1608–1674)

Evening

May the cross of the Son of God,
which is mightier than all the hosts of Satan
and more glorious than all the hosts of heaven,
abide with me in my going out and my coming in.
By day and night, . . . at all times and in all places
may it protect and defend me.
From the wrath of evildoers,
from the assaults of evil spirits,
from foes visible and invisible,
from the snares of the devil,
from all passions that beguile the soul and body:
may it guard, protect, and deliver me.
Amen.

—Church of India, Pakistan, Burma, and Ceylon

July 9

Morning

Blessed art Thou, O Lord,
our God, the God of our Fathers;
who turnest the shadow of death into the morning,
and renewest the face of the earth;
who removest darkness from the face of the light,
and banishest night, and bringest back the day;
Thou who hast lightened mine eyes,
that I sleep not in death;
who hast delivered me from the terror by night,
from the pestilence that walketh in darkness;
who hast driven sleep from mine eyes
and slumber from mine eyelids;
who makest the outgoings of the morning
and evening to rejoice;
for that I laid me down and slept and rose up again,
for the Lord sustained me. . . .
grant me to become a child of light, a child of the day,
to walk soberly, purely, honestly, as in the day.
Vouchsafe to keep me this day without sin.
Amen.

—Lancelot Andrewes (1555–1626)

Evening

God, of Your goodness, give me Yourself,
for You are sufficient for me. . . .
If I were to ask for anything less
I should always be in want,
for in You alone do I have all.
Amen.

—Julian of Norwich (c. 1342–1413)

July 10

Morning

Help us, O God,
to serve Thee devoutly
and the world busily.
May we do our work wisely,
give succour secretly,
go to our meat appetitely,
sit thereat discreetly,
arise temperately,
please our friend duly,
go to our bed merrily
and sleep surely,
for the joy of our Lord Jesus Christ.
Amen.

—Sulpicius Severus (c. 363–420)

Evening

Send Thy peace into my heart, O Lord, at the evening hour,
that I may be contented with Thy mercies of this day,
and confident of Thy protection for this night;
and now, having forgiven others,
even as Thou dost forgive me,
may I have a pure comfort and a healthful rest
within the shelter of this home;
through Jesus Christ our Saviour.
Amen.

—Henry van Dyke (1852–1933)

July 11

Morning

My God, I do not know what must come to me today.
But I am certain that nothing can happen to me
that You have not foreseen,
decreed, and ordained from all eternity.
That is sufficient for me.
I adore your impenetrable and eternal designs,
to which I submit with all my heart.
I desire, I accept them all, and I unite my sacrifice
to that of Jesus Christ, my divine Savior.
I ask in His name and through His infinite merits,
patience in my trials, and perfect and entire submission
to all that comes to me by Your good pleasure.
Amen.

—Joseph Pignatelli (1737–1811)

Evening

The Sacred Three
To save,
To shield,
To surround
The hearth,
The house,
The household
This eve,
This night,
And every night,
Each single night.
Amen.

—Traditional Gaelic prayer

July 12

Morning

Almighty God,
give me wisdom to perceive You,
intelligence to understand You,
diligence to seek You,
patience to wait for You,
eyes to behold You,
a heart to meditate upon You
and life to proclaim You,
through the power of the Spirit of our Lord Jesus Christ.
Amen.

—BENEDICT OF NURSIA (c. 480–543)

Evening

Before I go to rest, I would commit myself to God's care through Christ,
beseeching Him to forgive me for all my sins of this day past,
and to keep alive His grace in my heart,
and to cleanse me from all sin, pride, harshness, and selfishness,
and give me the spirit of meekness, humility, firmness, and love.
O Lord, keep Thyself present to me ever,
and perfect Thy strength in my weakness.
Take me and mine under Thy blessed care this night and evermore;
through Jesus Christ our Lord.
Amen.

—FREDERICK DENISON MAURICE (1805–1872)

Morning

Praised be Thou, O God,
who dost make the day bright with Thy sunshine,
and the night bright with the beam of heavenly fires.
Listen now to my prayers.
Watch over me with Thy power,
give me grace to pass this day of my life blamelessly,
free from sin and fear.
For with Thee is mercy
and plenteous redemption,
O Lord, my God.
Amen.

—GREEK LITURGY

Evening

Be present, O merciful God,
and protect me through the silent hours of this night,
so that I who am fatigued by the changes and chances
of this fleeting world,
may repose upon Thy eternal changelessness;
through Jesus Christ, the same yesterday, today and forever.
Amen.

—LEONINE SACRAMENTARY (5TH C.)

July 14

Morning

O Lord, give Your blessing, I pray, to my daily work,
that I may do it in faith and heartily, as to the Lord and not to men.
All my powers of body and mind are Yours,
and I devote them to Your service.
Sanctify them, and the work in which I am engaged;
and, Lord, so bless my efforts
that they may bring forth in me the fruits of true wisdom. . . .
Amen.

—THOMAS ARNOLD (1795–1842)

Evening

Bless us, O God the Father,
who hast created us,
Bless us, O God the Son,
who hast redeemed us,
Bless us, O God the Holy Ghost,
who sanctifieth us.
O Blessed Trinity,
keep us in body, soul, and spirit unto everlasting life.
Amen.

—WEIMARISCHES GESANGBUCH (1873)

JULY 15

Morning

Teach me, gracious Lord,
to begin my deeds with reverence,
to go on with obedience,
and to finish them in love;
and then to wait patiently in hope
and with cheerful confidence to look up to You,
whose promises are faithful and rewards infinite;
through Jesus Christ.
Amen.

—GEORGE HICKES (1642–1715)

Evening

May God the Father bless us;
may Christ take care of us;
the Holy Ghost enlighten us all the days of our life.
The Lord be our defender and keeper of body and soul,
both now and for ever,
to the ages of ages.
Amen.

—AETHELWOLD (c. 908–984)

Morning

Give me, good Lord,
a full faith,
a firm hope
and a fervent charity,
a love for Thee
incomparably above the
love of myself.
Amen.

—SIR THOMAS MORE (1478–1535)

Evening

And now, O blessed Redeemer,
my rock, my hope, and only sure defence,
to Thee do I cheerfully commit both my soul and body.
If Thy wise providence see fit,
grant that I may rise in the morning, refreshed with sleep,
and with a spirit of activity for the duties of the day,
but whether I wake here or in eternity
grant that my trust in Thee may remain sure,
and my hope unshaken,
through Jesus Christ our Lord.
Amen.

—HENRY KIRKE WHITE (1785–1806)

July 17

Morning

Worthy of praise from every mouth,
of confession from every tongue,
of worship from every creature,
is Thy glorious name, O Father, Son, and Holy Ghost:
who didst create the world in Thy grace
and by Thy compassion didst save the world.
To Thy majesty, O God, ten thousand times ten thousand
bow down and adore, singing and praising without ceasing and saying,
Holy, holy, holy, Lord God of hosts;
Heaven and earth are full of Thy praises;
Hosanna in the highest.
Amen.

—Nestorian Liturgy (5th c.)

Evening

O Lord our God,
in Your great goodness and in the richness of Your mercy
You have protected me . . . from the test of evil;
You who are the Creator of all things,
bring me safely to the time
when I offer You my prayers at daybreak,
and together with Your gift of true light
pour out in my heart the treasure of knowing You
that enables me to do Your will.
For You, O God, are good and loving to all mankind,
and I give You the glory, Father, Son and Holy Spirit,
now and for ever, to the ages of ages.
Amen.

—Eastern Orthodox Liturgy

July 18

Morning

Holy, holy, holy! Lord God Almighty!
Early in the morning our song shall rise to Thee;
Holy, holy, holy, merciful and mighty!
God in three Persons, blessed Trinity!

. . .

Holy, holy, holy! All the saints adore Thee,
Casting down their golden crowns around the glassy sea;
Cherubim and seraphim falling down before Thee,
Who wert, and art, and evermore shall be.

. . .

Holy, holy, holy! Lord God Almighty!
All Thy works shall praise Thy name, in earth, and sky, and sea;
Holy, holy, holy; merciful and mighty!
God in three Persons, blessed Trinity!
Amen.

—Reginald Heber (1783–1826)

Evening

May God the Father who made us bless us.
May God the Son send His healing among us.
May God the Holy Spirit move within us and give us
eyes to see with, ears to hear with, and hands
that Your work might be done.
May we walk and preach the word of God to all.
May the angel of peace watch over us and lead us at last
by God's grace to the Kingdom.
Amen.

—Dominic (1170–1221)

July 19

Morning

O God, the King eternal,
who dividest the day from
the darkness, and turnest the
shadow of death into the morning:
drive far off from me all wrong desires,
incline my heart to keep Thy law,
and guide my feet into the way of peace;
that having done Thy will with
cheerfulness while it was day,
I may, when the night cometh,
rejoice to give Thee thanks;
through Jesus Christ our Lord.
Amen.

—*Book of Common Prayer* (1928)

Evening

Lord, You are closer to me
than my own breathing,
nearer than my hands and feet.
Amen.

—*Teresa of Ávila* (1515–1582)

July 20

Morning

Dear Lord Jesus,
I shall have this day only once; before it is gone,
help me to do all the good I can,
so that today is not a wasted day.
Amen.

—Stephen Grellet (1773–1855)

Evening

Jesus Christ my God,
I adore You and I thank You for all the graces You have given me this day.
I offer You my sleep and all the moments of this night,
and I implore You to keep me safe from sin.
To this end I place myself in Your sacred side. . . .
Let Your holy angels surround me
and keep me in peace;
and let Your blessing be upon me.
Amen.

—Alphonsus de Liguori (1696–1787)

Morning

Jesus:
I want to unite my life to Your life,
my thoughts to Your thoughts,
my affections to Your affections,
my heart to Your heart,
my work to Your works,
my whole self to Your whole self,
in order to become through this union
more holy and more pleasing in the sight of Your Father,
and in order to make my life more worthy of Your grace
and of the reward of eternity.
I want to join Your intentions to my intentions,
the holiness of Your actions to mine,
and the excellence of Your lofty virtues to the lowliness of mine . . .
and when, in some one of my works,
I discover something not inspired by Your spirit
and which proceeds rather from my self-centeredness
or from some poorly mortified affection,
I will renounce it and disown it with my whole heart.
No, my Jesus, I promise myself to have nothing in me
which is not in union with Your lofty virtues.
Amen.

—Jean-Pierre Médaille (1610–1669)

Evening

Sleep, my soul, and peace attend Thee, all through the night;
Guardian angels God will send Thee, all through the night.
Slow the drowsy hours are creeping,
Hill and vale in slumber sleeping,
God His loving vigil keeping,
All through the night.
Amen.

—Welsh folk song

July 22

Morning

Grant to me, my Lord, that with peace of mind I may face
all that this new day is to bring.
Grant me grace to surrender myself completely to Your holy will.
For every hour of this day instruct and prepare me in all things.
Whatsoever tidings I may receive during the day,
do You teach me to accept tranquilly,
in the firm conviction that all my eventualities fulfill Your holy will.
Govern my thoughts and feelings in all I do and say.
When things unforeseen occur,
let me not forget that all comes down from You.
Teach me to behave sincerely and reasonably
toward every member of my family,
that I may bring confusion and sorrow to none.
Bestow on me, my Lord, strength to endure the fatigue of the day
and to bear my part in all its passing events.
Guide my will and teach me to pray, to believe, to hope,
to suffer, to forgive, and to love.
Amen.

—The Optina Elders (19th c.)

Evening

Into Thine arms I now commend myself this night.
I will lay me down in peace,
if Thou speak peace to me through Jesus Christ.
May my last thoughts be of Thee.
And when I awake, may Thy Spirit bring heavenly things to my mind.
Pardon the imperfections of my prayers.
Supply what I have omitted to ask for,
and do for me exceeding abundantly above all that I ask or think;
for the merits of Jesus Christ our Lord.
Amen.

—Fielding Ould (19th c.)

Morning

Eternal God,
I have many plans for today.
But I do not know what
the day will bring, despite my plans.
And more—I am but a mist.
I appear for a little while—
and then vanish.
My life here is a moment,
but You are eternal.
May I embark upon this day
intentional about what I think
You want me to do,
and yet humble about the limits of my plans,
my knowledge, my control.
Into Your hands I commit my day.
Amen.

—David P. Gushee (1962–)

Evening

Do not cast me off because I am a sinner,
do not hold aloof from me because I am not clean. . . .
Forgive the sins I have committed today.
Protect me during the coming night and keep me safe
from the machinations and contrivances of the enemy,
that I may not sin . . .
Amen.

—Macarius of Egypt (c. 300–390)

July 24

Morning

My good Lord,
another day is beginning outside,
the curtain going up on another blue-sky'd day.
Each day is Yours, a beautiful new scene in this play
You're staging of life on Earth.
You are directing it, yes,
but You are not its sole playwright.
You allow us men and women to come on Your stage and act,
affecting the script.
Our lines and actions can advance or hinder the course of Your drama.
Still I believe, Lord,
that the direction of this world is firmly in Your hands.
When the final curtain goes down
it will be upon the climactic scene of Your envisioning.
Beneficent Author of life,
let me play my part today,
in words and actions, so as to further Your plot on Earth,
and hasten the day when Your faithful
will enjoy a new Heaven and a new Earth.
Amen.

—JEANIE GUSHEE (1962–)

Evening

O blessed Jesus, give me stillness of soul in Thee.
Let Thy mighty calmness reign in me;
rule me, O King of Gentleness, King of peace. . . .
By Thine own deep patience, give me patience.
Make me in this and all things more and more like Thee.
Amen.

—JOHN OF THE CROSS (1542–1591)

Morning

O Heavenly Father,
in whom we live and move and have our being,
I humbly pray Thee so to guide and govern me by Thy Holy Spirit,
that in all the cares and occupations of my daily life
I may never forget Thee,
but remember that I am ever walking in Thy sight;
for Thine own name's sake.
Amen.

—ANCIENT COLLECT

Evening

Most high, omnipotent, righteous Lord,
to You be all praise, glory,
the honour and all blessing. . . .
Praise be to You, my Lord, for Sister Moon and the stars.
In heaven You fashioned them, clear and precious and beautiful. . . .
Praise be to You, my Lord,
for those who forgive sins in Your love,
and for those who bear sickness and tribulation.
Blessed are those who endure in peace,
for by You, most high Lord, they will be crowned.
Amen.

—FRANCIS OF ASSISI (1181–1226)

July 26

Morning

O Lord my God,
teach my heart . . . where and how to find You.
Lord, if You are not here but absent, where shall I seek You?
But You are everywhere,
so You must be here,
why then do I seek You? . . .
Lord, I am not trying to make my way to Your height,
for my understanding is in no way equal to that,
but I do desire to understand a little of Your truth,
which my heart already believes and loves.
I do not seek to understand so that I may believe,
but I believe so that I may understand;
and what is more,
I believe that unless I do believe I shall not understand.
Amen.

—ANSELM OF CANTERBURY (1033–1109)

Evening

O Lord God,
who has given us the night for rest,
I pray that in my sleep my soul may remain awake to You,
steadfastly adhering to Your love.
As I lay aside my cares to relax and relieve my mind,
may I not forget Your infinite and unresting care for me.
And in this way, let my conscience be at peace,
so that when I rise tomorrow, I am refreshed in body, mind and soul.
Amen.

—JOHN CALVIN (1509–1564)

July 27

Morning

Look upon me, O Lord,
and let all the darkness of my soul
vanish before the beams of Thy brightness.
Fill me with holy love,
and open to me the treasures of Thy wisdom.
All my desires are known unto Thee,
therefore perfect what Thou hast begun,
and what Thy Spirit has awakened me to ask for in prayer.
I seek Thy face;
turn Thy face unto me and show me Thy glory.
Then shall my longing be satisfied, and my peace shall be perfect.
Amen.

—Augustine of Hippo (354–430)

Evening

O Lord,
give me the strength that waits upon You in silence and in peace.
Give me humility, in which alone is rest,
and deliver me from pride, which is the heaviest of burdens.
Amen.

—Thomas Merton (1915–1968)

Morning

Give me, O Lord, a steadfast heart, which no selfish desires
may drag downwards;
give me an upright heart, which no unworthy ambitions
may tempt aside.
Give me also, O Lord my God, understanding to know You. . . .
through Jesus Christ our Lord.
Amen.

—THOMAS AQUINAS (1225–1274)

Evening

Ere I sleep, for every favour
This day showed
By my God
I will bless my Saviour.
O my Lord, what shall I render
To Thy name,
Still the same,
Merciful and tender?
Thou hast ordered all my goings
In Thy way,
Heard me pray,
Sanctified my doings. . . .
Thou my rock, my guard, my tower,
Safely keep,
While I sleep,
Me, with all Thy power. . . .
Amen.

—JOHN CENNICK (1718–1755)

Morning

O God, animate me to cheerfulness.
May I have a joyful sense of my blessings,
learn to look on the bright circumstances of my lot,
and maintain a perpetual contentedness.
Preserve me from despondency and from yielding to dejection.
Teach me that nothing can hurt me if, with true loyalty of affection,
I keep Your commands and take refuge in You.
Amen.

—William Ellery Channing (1780–1842)

Evening

Holy Father,
keep us in Your truth;
holy Son, protect us under the wings of Your cross;
Holy Spirit, make us temples and dwelling places for Your glory;
grant us Your peace all the days of our lives, O Lord.
Amen.

—Maronite Uniat Church prayer

JULY 30

Morning

God be in my head,
and in my understanding;
God be in my eyes,
and in my looking;
God be in my mouth,
and in my speaking;
God be in my heart,
and in my thinking;
God be at my end,
and at my departing.
Amen.

—SARUM PRIMER (16TH C.)

Evening

I commend unto You, O Lord,
my soul and my body,
my mind and my thoughts,
my prayers and my hopes,
my health and my work,
my life and my death,
my parents and brothers and sisters,
my benefactors and friends,
my neighbors, my countrymen,
and all Christian folk,
this day and always.
Amen.

—LANCELOT ANDREWES (1555–1626)

July 31

Morning

O Lord, lift up the light of Thy countenance upon me;
let peace rule in my heart,
and may it be my strength and my song,
in the house of my pilgrimage.
I commit myself to Thy care and keeping this day.
Let Thy grace be mighty in me, and sufficient for me,
and let it work in me both to will and to do Thine own good pleasure,
and grant me strength for all the duties of the day.
Amen.

—Matthew Henry (1662–1714)

Evening

Abide with me, O most blessed and merciful Savior,
for it is toward evening and the day is far spent.
As long as Thou art present with me,
I am in the light.
When Thou art present all is brightness,
all is sweetness.
I discourse with Thee, watch with Thee,
live with Thee, and lie down with Thee.
Abide then with me, O Thou whom my soul loveth;
Thou Son of righteousness with healing under Thy wings,
arise in my heart;
make Thy light then to shine in darkness
as a perfect day in the dead of night.
Amen.

—Henry Vaughan (1621–1695)

AUGUST 1

Morning

Let Thy blessing, O Lord, rest upon my work this day.
Teach me to seek after truth, and enable me to attain it;
but grant that as I increase in the knowledge of earthly things,
I may grow likewise in knowledge of Thee, whom to know is life eternal;
through Jesus Christ our Lord.
Amen.

—THOMAS ARNOLD (1795–1842)

Evening

When I look at Your heavens,
according to my own lights,
with these weak eyes of mine,
I am certain without reservation
that they are Your heavens.
The stars circle in the heavens,
reappear year after year,
each with a function and service to fulfill.
And though I do not understand them,
I know that You, O God, are in them.
Amen.

—HILARY OF POITIERS (c. 300–368)

AUGUST 2

Morning

Lord, be with me this day,
Within me to purify me;
Above me to draw me up;
Beneath me to sustain me;
Before me to lead me;
Behind me to restrain me;
Around me to protect me.
Amen.

—PATRICK OF IRELAND (c. 387–c. 460)

Evening

O Trinity, my all,
You are the immensity in which I can lose myself,
the Almighty Power to which I can surrender,
the holy ground in which I can bury myself,
the infinitely beautiful light
which I can contemplate for all eternity.
Amen.

—ELIZABETH CATEZ (1880–1906)

Morning

Rule over me this day, O God,
leading me on the path of righteousness.
Put Your Word in my mind and Your truth in my heart,
that this day I neither think nor feel anything
except what is good and honest. . . .
Let my eyes always look straight ahead on the road You wish me to tread,
that I might not be tempted by any distraction.
Amen.

—JACOB BOEHME (1575–1624)

Evening

Almighty and eternal God,
who hast revealed Thy nature in Christ Jesus Thy Son as love,
we humbly pray Thee:
give us Thy Holy Spirit to glorify Thee also in our hearts as pure love,
and thus constrain us by Thy divine power
to love Thee with our whole souls,
and our brethren as ourselves;
that so by Thy grace we may be fulfilled with love,
and evermore abide in Thee, and Thou in us,
with all joyfulness, and free from fear or distrust;
through Jesus Christ our Lord.
Amen.

—CHRISTIAN K. J. BUNSEN (1791–1860)

August 4

Morning

O God, You are my God;
Early will I seek You;
My soul thirsts for You;
My flesh longs for You
In a dry and thirsty land
Where there is no water.
So I have looked for You in the sanctuary,
To see Your power and Your glory.
Because Your lovingkindness is better than life,
My lips shall praise You.
Thus I will bless You while I live;
I will lift up my hands in Your name.
Amen.

—Psalm 63:1–4

Evening

O sweetest love of God, too little known,
whoever has found You will be at rest.
Let everything change, O my God,
that I may rest in You.
How sweet to me is Your presence, You who are the sovereign good!
I will draw near to You in silence. . . .
I will rejoice in nothing until I am in Your arms;
O Lord, I beseech You, leave me not for a moment.
Amen.

—John of the Cross (1542–1591)

Morning

Glorious Lord, I give You greeting!
Let the church and the chancel praise You,
Let the plains and the hillside praise You,
Let the dark and the daylight praise You. . . .
Let the life everlasting praise You!
Let the birds and the bees praise You,
Let the males and the females praise You,
Let the seven days of the week and the stars praise You. . . .
Let the books and the letters praise You. . . .
Let thought and action praise You. . . .
Let all the good that is created praise You.
And I too shall praise You, Lord of glory:
Glorious Lord, I give You greeting!
Amen.

—ANONYMOUS WELSH PRAYER (c. 10TH c.)

Evening

O God, I praise You for the night and for sleep.
Release my limbs of toil. Smooth my brow of care.
Grant me a refreshing draught of forgetfulness.
Comfort those who toss on a bed of pain,
or whose nerves crave sleep and find it not.
Save them from despondent thoughts in the darkness.
May they learn to lean on Your all-pervading life and love,
so their souls may grow tranquil and their bodies may rest.
Amen.

—WALTER RAUSCHENBUSCH (1861–1918)

August 6

Morning

O God, from whom all holy desires,
all good counsels, and all just works proceed:
give unto me, Thy servant,
today that peace which the world cannot give,
that my heart may be set to obey Thy commandments,
and that I may pass my time this day in restful quietness of spirit;
through the merits of Jesus Christ our Savior.
Amen.

—Book of Common Prayer (1863)

Evening

Almighty Father, Son and Holy Spirit, eternal and ever-blessed God;
to me the least of saints, to me allow that I may keep a door in Paradise.
That I may keep even the smallest, the furthest, the darkest, coldest door,
the door that is least used, the stiffest door.
If so it but be in Your house, O God,
if so be that I can see Your glory even from afar,
and hear Your voice, O God,
and know that I am with You, O God,
through Jesus Christ our Lord.
Amen.

—Columba of Ireland (c. 521–597)

Morning

I offer You, Lord, my thoughts to be fixed on You;
my words to have You for their theme;
my actions to reflect my love for You;
my sufferings to be endured for Your greater glory.
I want to do what You ask of me:
in the way You ask,
for as long as You ask,
because You ask it.
Lord, enlighten my understanding,
strengthen my will,
purify my heart,
and make me holy.
Amen.

—POPE CLEMENT XI (1649–1721)

Evening

Come, Lord, and cover me with the night.
Spread Your grace over us as You assured us You would do.
Your promises are more than all the stars in the sky;
Your mercy is deeper than the night. . . .
The night comes with its breath of death.
Night comes, the end comes,
but Jesus Christ comes also.
Lord, we wait for Him day and night.
Amen.

—PRAYER FROM WEST AFRICA

AUGUST 8

Morning

O Master, Lord, God the Almighty,
I thank You for every condition, . . . and in every condition,
for You have covered me, helped me, guarded me, accepted me unto You,
spared me, supported me, and brought me to this hour.
Therefore I . . . entreat Your goodness, O Lover of mankind, to grant me
to complete this holy day, and all the days of my life, in all peace. . . .
All temptation, all the works of Satan . . . take them away from me. . . .
But those things which are good and profitable do provide for me. . . .
By the grace, compassion and love of mankind
of Your only begotten Son Jesus Christ,
through whom the glory, the honor, the dominion, and the adoration
are due unto You, with Him and the Holy Spirit, the Life-Giver,
now and unto the ages of ages.
Amen.

—COPTIC ORTHODOX PRAYER

Evening

Visit this place, O Lord,
and drive far from it all snares of the enemy;
let Your holy angels dwell with us to preserve us in peace;
and let Your blessing be upon us always;
through Jesus Christ our Lord.
Amen.

—BOOK OF COMMON PRAYER (1979)

August 9

Morning

O Lord,
grant me to greet the coming day in peace.
Help me in all things to rely upon Thy holy will.
In every hour of the day reveal Thy will to me.
Bless my dealings with all who surround me.
In all my deeds and words guide my thoughts and feelings.
Teach me to act firmly and wisely,
without embittering or embarrassing others.
Give me strength to bear the fatigue of Thy coming day
with all that it shall bring.
Direct my will, teach me to pray,
pray Thou Thyself in me.
Amen.

—Drizdov Philaret (1782–1867)

Evening

Lord, make me according to Thy heart.
Amen.

—Brother Lawrence (1611–1691)

Morning

Lord, Thou knowest better than I know myself
that I am growing older and will some day be old.
Keep me from the fatal habit of thinking that I must say something
on every subject and every occasion.
Release me from craving to straighten out everybody's affairs.
Make me thoughtful but not moody; helpful but not bossy.
With my vast store of wisdom, it seems a pity not to use it all,
but Thou knowest, Lord, that I want a few friends at the end. . . .
Seal my lips on my aches and pains,
for love of rehearsing them will become sweeter as the years go by. . . .
Teach me the glorious lesson that occasionally I may be wrong.
Keep me reasonably sweet . . .
a sour old person is one of the crowning works of the devil.
Give me the ability to see good things in unexpected places,
and talents in unexpected people.
And give me, O Lord, the grace to tell them so.
Amen.

—Anonymous (attributed to a nun) (17th c.)

Evening

O God, who gives the day for work and the night for sleep,
refresh my body and my mind
through the quiet hours of night,
and let my inward eyes be directed towards You,
dreaming of Your eternal glory.
Amen.

—Leonine Sacramentary (5th c.)

August 11

Morning

When the day returns, call us with morning faces,
and with morning hearts,
eager to labor,
happy if happiness be our portion,
and if the day is marked for sorrow, strong to endure.
Amen.

—ROBERT LOUIS STEVENSON (1850–1894)

Evening

Almighty God, You are Lord of time
and have neither beginning nor end:
You are the redeemer of our souls,
the foundation of human reason
and guardian of our hearts;
through all that You have created
You have revealed Your indescribable power;
receive, O Lord, our supplication
even at this hour of the night,
provide fully for the needs of each one of us
and make us worthy of Your goodness.
For Your Name
is worthy of all honor and greatness
and is to be glorified with hymns of blessing,
Father, Son and Holy Spirit,
now and for ever,
to the ages of ages.
Amen.

—GREEK ORTHODOX PRAYER (8TH C.)

Morning

O Lord,
give me more charity,
more self-denial,
more likeness to Thee.
Teach me to sacrifice my comforts to others,
and my likings for the sake of doing good.
Make me kindly in thought,
gentle in word, generous in deed.
Teach me that it is better to give than to receive . . .
And unto Thee, the God of Love, be glory
and praise for ever.
Amen.

—HENRY ALFORD (1810–1871)

Evening

The eternal kingdom is within sight,
a kingdom that shall suffer no loss.
Lord Jesus Christ, we are Christians,
we are Your servants;
You alone are our hope,
the hope of all Christians.
God almighty, God most high;
we give You praise,
we give praise to Your name.
Amen.

—THELICA OF ABITINE (D. 304)

AUGUST 13

Morning

O Lord,
I thank You for the beauties of this world You've made.
I pray that Your kingdom will come on earth
as You want it to, a kingdom of peace, justice, truth, and kindness.
Help me do what furthers that kingdom.
Let me walk before You today in righteousness,
and help me be productive in the tasks that are mine to perform.
Amen.

—JEANIE GUSHEE (1962–)

Evening

O God, the source of eternal light:
shed forth Thine unending day upon us who watch for Thee,
that our lips may praise Thee, our lives may bless Thee,
and our worship on the morrow may give Thee glory;
through Jesus Christ our Lord.
Amen.

—BOOK OF COMMON PRAYER (1979)

AUGUST 14

Morning

O God, my heart is steadfast;
I will sing and give praise, even with my glory.
Awake, lute and harp!
I will awaken the dawn.
I will praise You, O LORD, among the peoples,
And I will sing praises to You among the nations.
For Your mercy is great above the heavens,
And Your truth reaches to the clouds.
Be exalted, O God, above the heavens,
And Your glory above all the earth.
Amen.

—PSALM 108:1–5

Evening

Now as I lay down to sleep, O Master,
grant me repose both of body and of soul . . .
calm the commotions of my flesh
and put away all earthly and material thoughts as I sleep. . . .
And raise me up again at the hour of prayer,
established in Thy commandments
and holding steadfast within myself
the remembrance of Thy judgments. . . .
The Father is my hope;
the Son is my refuge;
the Holy Spirit is my shelter.
O Holy Trinity, glory to Thee.
Amen.

—EASTERN ORTHODOX PRAYER AT COMPLINE

Morning

Thanks be to Thee, O Lord Christ,
for all the benefits which Thou hast given us;
for all the pains and insults which Thou hast borne for us.
O most merciful Redeemer, friend, and brother,
may we know Thee more clearly,
love Thee more dearly,
and follow Thee more nearly;
for Thine own sake.
Amen.

—RICHARD OF CHICHESTER (1197–1253)

Evening

Preserve me, Lord, while I am waking,
and defend me while I am sleeping,
that my soul may continually watch for You,
and both body and soul may rest in Your peace forever.
Amen.

—JOHN COSIN (1594–1672)

Morning

O Eternal Godhead,
O sea profound,
what more could You give me than Yourself? . . .
With Your light You illuminate me so that I may know all Your truth.
Clothe me, clothe me with Your eternal truth,
so that I may run this mortal life with true obedience,
and with the light of Your most holy faith.
Amen.

—CATHERINE OF SIENA (1347–1380)

Evening

Our God, You open Your hand,
and fill all things living with plenteousness;
to You I commit all those who are dear to me;
watch over them, I pray,
and provide all things needful for their souls and bodies,
now and for evermore;
through Jesus Christ our Lord.
Amen.

—NERSES (4TH C.)

AUGUST 17

Morning

I pray to You, O Lord, who are the supreme Truth,
and all truth is from You.
I beseech You, O Lord, who are the highest Wisdom,
and all the wise depend on You for their wisdom.
You are the supreme Joy, and all who are happy owe it to You.
You are the highest Good, and all goodness comes from You.
You are the Light of minds, and all receive
their understanding from You.
I love You—indeed I love You above all things.
I seek You, follow You, and am prepared to serve You.
I desire to dwell under Your power, for You are the King of all.
Amen.

—KING ALFRED THE GREAT OF WESSEX (849–899)

Evening

O Lord, let me not henceforth desire health or life,
except to spend them for You, with You, and in You.
You alone know what is good for me;
do, therefore, what seems best to You.
Give to me, or take from me;
conform my will to Yours;
and grant that, with humble and perfect submission,
and in holy confidence,
I may receive the orders of Your eternal Providence;
and may equally adore all that comes to me from You;
through Jesus Christ our Lord.
Amen.

—BLAISE PASCAL (1623–1662)

Morning

Lord Jesus . . .
help me to cast out from my mind
all thoughts of which You do not approve
and from my heart all emotions which You do not encourage.
Enable me to spend my entire day as a coworker with You,
carrying out the tasks that You have entrusted to me.
Be with me at every moment of this day: during the long hours of work,
that I may never tire or slacken from Your service . . .
and during moments of worry and stress,
that I may remain patient and spiritually calm.
Amen.

—*Catholic Book of Prayers* (2005)

Evening

By night I lift up my hands to the holy place, and praise the Lord.
The Lord hath granted His loving-kindness in the day-time;
and in the night season will I sing of Him,
and make my prayer unto the God of my life.
As long as I live I will magnify Thee in this manner,
and lift up my hands in Thy name.
Let my prayer be set forth in Thy sight as incense,
and let the lifting up of my hands be an evening sacrifice.
Blessed art Thou, O Lord, . . .
who has not cut off like the weaver my life,
nor from morning even to night made an end of me.
Amen.

—Lancelot Andrewes (1555–1626)

Morning

O Lord our God,
give me by Your Holy Spirit
a willing heart and a ready hand
to use all Your gifts to Your praise and glory;
through Jesus Christ our Lord.
Amen.

—THOMAS CRANMER (1489–1556)

Evening

Sunk is the sun's last beam of light,
And now the world is wrapped in night.
Christ, light us with Thy heavenly ray,
Nor let our feet in darkness stray.
Thanks, Lord, that Thou throughout the day
Hast kept all grief and harm away;
That angels tarried round about
Our coming in and going out.
Whate'er of wrong we've done or said,
Let not the charge on us be laid,
That, through Thy free forgiveness blest,
In peaceful slumber we may rest.
Thy guardian angels round us place
All evil from our couch to chase;
Our soul and body, while we sleep,
In safety, gracious Father, keep.
Amen.

—NICOLAUS HERMAN (c. 1480–1561);
TRANSLATED BY FRANCES COX (1812–1897)

Morning

Give me, good Lord, an humble, lowly, quiet,
peaceable, patient, charitable, kind, tender, and pity-filled mind,
with all my works, and all my words, and all my thoughts,
to have a taste of Thy holy, blessed Spirit. . . .
Take from me, good Lord, this lukewarm fashion,
or rather key-cold manner of meditation,
and this dullness in praying unto Thee.
And give me warmth, delight and quickness in thinking upon Thee.
The things, good Lord, that I pray for, give me Thy grace to labor for.
Amen.

—Sir Thomas More (1478–1535)

Evening

Father, You are love, and You see all the suffering,
injustice and misery which reign in this world.
Have pity, we implore You, on the work of Your hands.
Look mercifully on the poor, the oppressed, and all who are heavy laden
with error, labor and sorrow.
Fill our hearts with deep compassion for those who suffer,
and hasten the coming of Your kingdom of justice and truth,
through Jesus Christ our Lord.
Amen.

—Eugene Bersier (1831–1889)

Morning

Father in Heaven! Reawaken conscience in my breast.
Make me bend the ear of the spirit to Thy voice,
so that I may perceive Thy will for me in its clear purity,
as it is in Heaven, pure of my false worldly wisdom,
unstifled by the voice of passion. . . .
Grant that I may hear also a gentle voice murmuring to me
that I am Thy child,
so I will cry with joy, "Abba, Father!"
Amen.

—SØREN KIERKEGAARD (1813–1855)

Evening

Take me, I pray Thee,
O Lord of my life,
into Thy keeping this night and for ever.
O Thou light of lights,
keep me from inward darkness;
grant me so to sleep in peace,
that I may arise to work according to Thy will;
through Jesus Christ our Lord.
Amen.

—LANCELOT ANDREWES (1555–1626)

Morning

In this hour of this day, fill me, O Lord, with Your mercy;
that rejoicing throughout the whole day,
I may take delight in Your praise;
through Jesus Christ our Lord.
Amen.

—SARUM MISSAL (16TH C.)

Evening

Now the day is over, night is drawing nigh;
Shadows of the evening steal across the sky . . .
Jesus, give the weary calm and sweet repose;
With Thy tenderest blessing may mine eyelids close. . . .
Through the long night-watches
May Thine angels spread
Their white wings above me,
Watching round my bed.
When the morning wakens, then may I arise
Pure and fresh and sinless in Thy holy eyes.
Amen.

—SABINE BARING-GOULD (1834–1924)

Morning

And now, Lord, what wait I for?
My hope is in You.
Do more for me than I can possibly ask or think,
and finally receive me to Yourself.
Amen.

—Maria W. Stewart (1803–1879)

Evening

In Thy name, O Jesu who wast crucified,
I lie down to rest;
watch Thou me in sleep remote.
Hold Thou me in Thy one hand.
Bless me, O my Christ,
be Thou my shield protecting me,
aid my steps in the pitiful swamp,
lead Thou me to the life eternal.
Keep Thou me in the presence of God,
O good and gracious Son of the Virgin,
and fervently I pray Thy strong protection
from my lying down at dusk to my rising at day.
Amen.

—Celtic prayer

Morning

O Thou most holy and everloving God . . .
While we have slept, the world in which we live has swept on in its awful space,
great fires have burned under us,
great waters have been all about us, and great storms above us;
but Thou hast held them back by Thy strong hand,
and we have rested under the shadow of Thy love.
The bird sat on the spray out in the darkness, the flower nestled in the grass,
we lay down in our home,
and all slept in the arms of God.
The bird will trust Thee this day to give its morsel of meat,
and the flower will trust Thee for its fresh raiment;
so may I trust Thee this day for all the needs of the body, the soul, and the spirit.
Give us this day our daily bread.
Amen.

—ROBERT COLLYER (1823–1912)

Evening

O Lord our God, I come to You now with open heart
to call upon Your holy name
and to give You thanks for keeping me safe during this day
and for bringing me to the light of evening.
I pray that this evening and the approaching night
and all the days of my earthly life may be free from sin:
clothe me with the armor of Your Holy Spirit
to fight against the forces of evil and the passions of the flesh;
put far from me all sin and make me worthy of Your eternal kingdom.
For to You belong all glory, honor and praise,
Father, Son and Holy Spirit,
now and for ever, to the ages of ages.
Amen.

—EASTERN ORTHODOX PRAYER

Morning

Lord, may I be wakeful at sunrise to begin a new day for you,
and cheerful at sunset for having done my work for you;
thankful at moonrise and under starshine for the beauty of the universe.
And may I add what little may be in me to your great world.
Amen.

—The Abbot of Greve (12th c.)

Evening

Blest be the God of love,
Who gave me eyes, and light, and power this day,
Both to be busy and to play. . . .
My God, Thou art all love.
Not one poor minute escapes Thy breast,
But brings a favor from above;
And in this love, more than in bed, I rest.
Amen.

—George Herbert (1593–1633)

August 26

Morning

O God, Creator of light:
at the rising of Your sun this morning,
let the greatest of all lights, Your Love,
rise like the sun within my heart.
Amen.

—Armenian Church

Evening

Grant, O God, Your protection;
and in Your protection, strength;
and in strength, understanding;
and in understanding, knowledge;
and in knowledge, the knowledge of justice;
and in the knowledge of justice, the love of it;
and in that love, the love of existence;
and in the love of all existence, the love of God,
God and all goodness.
Amen.

—Ancient Welsh prayer

Morning

I am not worthy, Lord and Master, that You should come under the roof
of my soul: nevertheless, since You desire, O lover of mankind,
to dwell within me, I am bold to draw near.
You invite me to open the door which You alone have made,
that entering in there You may bring light into my darkened mind:
I do believe that You will do this.
For You did not . . . reject the thief when he sought to enter Your kingdom,
nor did You reject the persecutor when he repented.
But You treated all who came to You in penitence as Your friends.
You alone are to be blessed, now and for ever.
Amen.

—JOHN CHRYSOSTOM (c. 347–407)

Evening

Keep us in peace, O Christ our God,
under the protection of Your holy and venerable Cross;
save us from enemies visible and invisible
and count us worthy to glorify You with thanksgiving,
with the Father and the Holy Spirit now and ever and world without end.
Amen.

—ARMENIAN ORTHODOX LITURGY

Morning

O Lord,
move my heart with the calm, smooth flow of Your grace.
Let the river of Your love run through my soul.
May my soul be carried by the current of Your love,
towards the wide, infinite ocean of heaven.
Stretch out my heart with Your strength,
as You stretch out the sky above the earth.
Smooth out any wrinkles of hatred or resentment.
Enlarge my soul that it may know more fully Your truth.
Amen.

—GILBERT OF HOYLAND (D. 1170)

Evening

Give me this night, O Father,
the peace of mind which is truly rest.
Take from me . . . all resentment for anything
which has been withheld from me;
all foolish worry about the future and all futile regret about the past.
Help me to be at peace with myself,
at peace with my fellow human beings,
at peace with You,
so indeed may I lay myself down to rest in peace,
through Jesus Christ my Lord.
Amen.

—ANONYMOUS

AUGUST 29

Open Your doors of mercy, Lord:
hear our prayer and have mercy upon our souls. . . .
Let Your light shine in our minds
and drive away the shadows of error and night.
The creation is full of light,
give Your light also to our hearts:
that we may praise You all the day long.
The morning and the evening praise You, Lord:
they bring You the praise of Your church.
Light which gives light to all creatures:
give light to our minds that we may thank You, Lord.
Amen.

—SYRIAN ORTHODOX PRAYER

Evening

Eternal Trinity, You are like a deep sea,
in which the more I seek,
the more I find;
and the more I find,
the more eagerly I seek.
You fill the soul, yet never fully satisfy it;
the soul continues to hunger and thirst for You,
desiring You, longing to see You who are the source of all light.
In Your light, eternal Trinity, I have seen into the deep ocean of Your love,
and have rejoiced in the beauty of Your creation. . . .
You are goodness beyond all goodness,
beauty beyond all beauty,
wisdom beyond all wisdom.
You are the garment that covers all nakedness.
You are the food that satisfies all hunger.
Amen.

—CATHERINE OF SIENA (1347–1380)

Morning

O Lord our God,
teach me, I beseech Thee, to ask Thee aright for the right things.
Steer Thou the vessel of my life towards Thyself,
Thou tranquil haven of all storm-tossed souls.
Show me the course wherein I should go.
Renew a willing spirit within me.
Let Thy Spirit curb my waywardness and guide and enable me
unto that which is my true good, to keep Thy laws,
and in all my works evermore
to rejoice in Thy glorious and gladdening presence.
For Thine is the glory and praise from all Thy saints for ever and ever.
Amen.

—Basil of Caesarea (c. 330–379)

Evening

Lord God:
Drop Thy still dews of quietness,
Till all our strivings cease;
Take from our souls the strain and stress,
And let our ordered lives confess
The beauty of Thy peace.
Amen.

—John Greenleaf Whittier (1807–1892)

Morning

Glory to the never-failing power of Your cross, O Lord!
When the enemy oppresses me with sinful thoughts and feelings,
and I turn my mind and my heart to You, nailed on the cross,
then my sin suddenly passes away,
the aggression lifts, and I am free.
Lord, let nothing carnal, nothing evil, turn me away from You.
Let me always be with You.
How good it is to be with You.
Amen.

—JOHN SERGIEFF (1829–1908)

Evening

O Christ, give us patience and faith and hope
as we kneel at the foot of Thy Cross,
and hold fast to it.
Teach us by Thy Cross that however ill the world may be,
the Father so loved us that He spared not Thee.
Amen.

—CHARLES KINGSLEY (1819–1875)

September 1

Morning

Holy Spirit, the life that gives life,
You are the cause of all movement;
You are the breath of all creatures;
You are the salve that purifies our souls;
You are the ointment that heals our wounds;
You are the fire that warms our hearts;
You are the light that guides our feet.
Let all the world praise You!
Amen.

—Hildegard of Bingen (1098–1179)

Evening

You are the Wisdom, uncreated and eternal,
the supreme first cause, above all being,
sovereign Godhead, sovereign goodness,
watching unseen the God-inspired wisdom of Christian people.
Raise us, we pray, that we may totally respond
to the supreme, unknown, ultimate, and splendid height
of Your words, mysterious and inspired.
Amen.

—*The Cloud of Unknowing* (14th c.)

Morning

Set my heart on fire with the love of Thee, most loving Father,
and then to do Thy will, and to obey Thy commandments,
will not be grievous to me.
For to him that loveth, nothing is difficult, nothing is impossible;
because love is stronger than death.
Oh, may love fill and rule my heart.
For then there will spring up and be cherished between Thee and me
a likeness of character and union of will,
so that I may choose and refuse what Thou dost.
May Thy will be done in me and by me for ever.
Amen.

—JACOBUS MERLO HORSTIUS (1597–1664)

Evening

My soul shall be satisfied . . .
And my mouth shall praise You with joyful lips.
When I remember You on my bed,
I meditate on You in the night watches.
Because You have been my help,
Therefore in the shadow of Your wings I will rejoice.
Amen.

—PSALM 63:5–7

Morning

Living Lord,
You have watched over me,
and put Your hand on my head
during the long, dark hours of night.
Your holy angels have protected me from all harm and pain.
To You, Lord, I owe life itself.
Continue to watch over me
and bless me during the hours of day.
Amen.

—JACOB BOEHME (1575–1624)

Evening

Blessed are You, eternal God,
King of the universe:
You have called us in Jesus to be Your beloved people,
living pure and blameless lives in Your sight.
Bless my family who ask for Your grace.
Let Your Spirit guide our words and deeds,
so that our light may shine before all
and lead all who know us to give You praise.
May our home be filled with the spirit of love,
with the obedience of faith,
and the strength of hope.
Make our lives happy in Your service,
and bring us in Your love to Your eternal home.
Father all-holy,
I praise Your Name,
and ask this blessing through Christ our Lord.
Amen.

—CATHOLIC PRAYER

Morning

Lord, I know not what I ought to ask of You.
You only know what I need.
You know me better than I know myself.
O Father, give to Your child what he himself knows not how to ask.
Teach me to pray. Pray Yourself in me.
Amen.

—FRANÇOIS FÉNELON (1651–1715)

Evening

Lord Jesus Christ,
Abide with us now that the sun has run its course.
Let hope not be obscured by night,
But may faith's darkness be as light.
Lord Jesus Christ, grant us Your peace,
And when the trials of earth shall cease,
Grant us the morning light of grace,
The radiant splendor of Your face.
Immortal, Holy, Three-fold Light,
Yours be the Kingdom, power and might,
All glory be eternally
To You, life-giving Trinity!
Amen.

—*MANE NOBISCUM DOMINE* (14TH c.)

September 5

Morning

Father, let me not be misled today
by the enticements of an age that is passing,
by entertainments, trends, and philosophies,
which are no more than so many dandelion seed-heads
which You shall blow away when it pleases You.
Rather, let me do Your will.
Amen.

—Jeanie Gushee (1962–)

Evening

Time has come for me to sleep,
And I thank Thee for Thy keep.
Watch this night well over me.
Teach me, Lord, to trust in Thee.
Many sins I've done today;
Please, Lord, take them all away.
Look upon me in Thy grace.
Make me pure before Thy face.
Care for those who are sick and poor;
Grant them, Lord, Thy blessing more.
Care for those I love the same.
This I pray in Jesus' name.
Amen.

—Anonymous children's prayer

September 6

Morning

O God, who are the Giver of all good gifts,
I Your unworthy servant entirely desire to praise Your name
for all the expressions of Your bounty toward me. . . .
Blessed be Your love for all the temporal benefits which You have
with a liberal hand poured out upon me;
for my health and strength, food and raiment,
and all other necessaries with which You
have provided Your sinful servant.
I also bless You, that after all my refusals of Your grace,
You still have patience with me, have . . . given me yet another day
to renew and perfect my repentance.
Make Yourself always present to my mind,
and let Your love fill and rule my soul,
in all those places, and companies, and employments
to which You call me this day.
Amen.

—John Wesley (1703–1791)

Evening

I know too well that I am weak and changeable.
I know the power of temptation against the strongest virtue.
I have seen stars fall and foundations of my world crack;
these things do not alarm me.
While I hope in You, I am sheltered from all misfortune,
and I am sure that my trust shall endure,
for I rely upon You to sustain this unfailing hope.
Finally, I know that my confidence cannot exceed Your generosity,
and that I shall never receive less than I have hoped for from You.
Amen.

—Claude La Colombière (1641–1682)

Morning

Shine upon my ways.
May I this day get nearer heaven.
May I feel at its close that I have done something for God—
something to promote the great end
for which existence was given me—
the glory of Thy holy name.
Amen.

—JOHN MACDUFF (1818–1895)

Evening

Lord, fill this night with Your radiance.
May I sleep in peace, and rise in joy,
to welcome the light of a new day in Your name.
I ask this through Christ our Lord.
Amen.

—THE DIVINE OFFICE

Morning

O Lord God, give me grace to set a good example
to all amongst whom I live,
to be just and true in all my dealings,
to be strict and conscientious in the discharge of every duty,
pure and temperate in all enjoyment,
kind and charitable and courteous toward all men;
that so the mind of Jesus Christ may be formed in me,
and all men take knowledge of me that I am His disciple;
through the same Jesus Christ our Lord.
Amen.

—CHARLES JOHN VAUGHAN (1816–1897)

Evening

Light of the world,
shine upon our minds and hearts.
Spirit of truth,
guide us into all truth.
Holy Father, sanctify us through Thy truth,
and make us wise unto salvation,
through Jesus Christ our Lord.
Amen.

—LAWRENCE TUTTIETT (1825–1897)

September 9

Morning

Lift up our hearts, O Christ, above the false shows of things,
above laziness and fear, above custom and fashion,
up to the everlasting Truth which is Thee Thyself;
so that we may live joyfully and freely,
in the faith that Thou art our King and our Savior,
our example and our judge;
and that, so long as we are loyal to Thee,
all will be well with us in this world and in all worlds to come,
O Jesus Christ our Lord.
Amen.

—Charles Kingsley (1819–1875)

Evening

Breathe in me, Holy Spirit, that I may think what is holy.
Move in me, Holy Spirit, that I may do what is holy.
Attract me, Holy Spirit, that I may love what is holy.
Strengthen me, Holy Spirit, that I may guard what is holy.
Guard me, Holy Spirit, that I may keep what is holy.
Amen.

—Augustine of Hippo (354–430)

Morning

Almighty God,
who in Thy wisdom hast so ordered our earthly life
that we needs must walk by faith and not by sight;
grant me such faith in Thee that,
amidst all things that pass my understanding,
I may believe in Thy fatherly care,
and ever be strengthened by the assurance
that underneath are the everlasting arms;
through Jesus Christ our Lord.
Amen.

—ANONYMOUS

Evening

O Lord our God,
who lives in unapproachable light,
in Your great mercy You have been my constant guide
throughout this day
and have called me to give You glory at eventide:
hear the prayer of Your unworthy servant
and keep me safe from the darkness of sin.
Give light to my soul
that being ever in awe of You and going forward in Your light
I may glorify You in all things
who in Your unfailing love for all mankind are the one true God.
For Yours is the greatness, the majesty,
the power and the glory,
Father, Son and Holy Spirit,
now and for ever,
to the ages of ages.
Amen.

—EASTERN ORTHODOX PRAYER AT COMPLINE

Morning

Grant me, O Lord, to pass this day in gladness and in peace,
without stumbling and without stain;
that, reaching the eventide victorious over all temptation,
I may praise thee,
the Eternal God, who art blessed,
and dost govern all things, world without end.
Amen.

—MOZARABIC LITURGY (7TH C.)

Evening

God to enfold me,
God to surround me,
God in my speaking,
God in my thinking.
God in my sleeping,
God in my waking,
God in my watching,
God in my hoping.
God in my life,
God in my lips,
God in my soul,
God in my heart.
God in my sufficing,
God in my slumber,
God in mine ever-living soul,
God in mine eternity.
Amen.

—*CARMINA GADELICA* (1900)

Morning

O Lord, give us grace not only to be hearers of the word,
but also doers of the same;
not only to love, but to live Thy gospel;
not only to profess, but also to practice Thy blessed commandments,
to the honor of Thy holy name.
Amen.

—Thomas Becon (c. 1512–1567)

Evening

O Thou God of peace,
unite our hearts by Thy bond of peace,
that we may live with one another continually
in gentleness and humility,
in peace and unity.
Amen.

—Bernhard Albrecht (1569–1636)

Morning

I rise and pledge myself, Lord,
that this day I shall do no evil deed,
but offer every moment as a sacrifice to You. . . .
I shudder to recall how I have betrayed You.
Yet You know that now I want only to serve You.
Make me this day Your devoted slave.
Amen.

—GREGORY OF NAZIANZUS (c. 325–389)

Evening

Dear Lord,
The people I encountered today
walk again before my mind's eye as day ends.
Loving God, I lift each one to You—
those whom I love, those whom I barely know,
those with whom I struggle.
Each one You made in Your divine image;
each You have sustained until this moment;
each You have suffered and died for in Your Son.
As my eyes close, I ask You to bless each one,
and may I be a blessing to them also,
tomorrow and in days to come.
Amen.

—DAVID P. GUSHEE (1962–)

September 14

Morning

Who can tell what a day might bring?
Therefore, gracious God,
cause me to live every day as if it were to be my last,
for I know not but that it may be such.
Cause me to live now,
as I shall wish I had done when I come to die.
Amen.

—Thomas à Kempis (1380–1471)

Evening

Bless those who breathe
In the stardust
Of night.
Bless those who rise
At the breaking
Of light.
Let us shine.
Let us shine.
Let us shine.
Amen.

—Peter Markus (1966–)

Morning

Lord, grant me a simple, kind, open,
believing, loving and generous heart,
worthy of being Your dwelling-place.
Amen.

—JOHN SERGIEFF (1829–1908)

Evening

God,
who by making the evening to succeed the day
has bestowed the gift of sleep on human weakness,
grant, I beseech You, that while I enjoy Your blessings
I may acknowledge Him from whom they came,
through Jesus Christ.
Amen.

—MOZARABIC SACRAMENTARY (7TH C.)

September 16

Morning

I thank You, God, that I have lived
In this great world and known its many joys;
The song of birds, the strong, sweet scent of hay
And cooling breezes in the secret dusk,
The flaming sunsets at the close of day,
Hills, and the lonely, heather-covered moors,
Music at night, and moonlight on the sea,
The beat of waves upon the rocky shore
And wild, white spray, flung high in ecstasy,
The faithful eyes of dogs, and treasured books.
The love of kin and fellowship of friends,
And all that makes life dear and beautiful. . . .
Because of these and other blessings poured
Unasked upon my wondering head,
Because I know that there is yet to come
An even richer and more glorious life,
And most of all, because Your only Son
Once sacrificed life's loveliness for me—
I thank You, God, that I have lived.
Amen.

—Elizabeth, Countess of Craven (1750–1828)

Evening

Dear Jesus,
as a hen covers her chicks with her wings to keep them safe,
do You this night protect us under Your golden wings.
Amen.

—Prayer from India

Morning

Lord Jesus Christ,
You are the sun that always rises,
but never sets. . . .
You are the source of all food,
material and spiritual,
nourishing us in both body and soul.
You are the light that dispels the clouds
of error and doubt,
and goes before me every hour of the day,
guiding my thoughts and my actions.
May I walk in your light,
be nourished by Your food,
be sustained by Your mercy,
and be warmed by Your love.
Amen.

—ERASMUS (1466–1536)

Evening

O God our Father,
utterly loving, utterly wise,
hold me this night within Your safekeeping.
At night men and women have long turned towards You;
I come with my own faults,
my own small faith, seeking more;
I bow before You in humility and wonder.
Let no experience of this day
hinder my true service, I pray.
Let Your kingdom come among men and women,
Your will be done.
Amen.

—RITA SNOWDEN (1907–1999)

September 18

Morning

O God, be all my love, all my hope, all my striving;
let my thoughts and words flow from You,
my daily life be in You,
and every breath I take be for You.
Amen.

—John Cassian (c. 360–435)

Evening

I pray Thee, O Creator of everything,
at this hour preceding night,
that Thou be clement and watch over me.
Let dreams and phantoms soften and be scattered.
Keep me safe from our enemy and make me pure!
Amen.

—Ambrose of Milan (339–397)

Morning

Lord, make me pure:
Only the pure shall see Thee as Thou art,
And shall endure.
Lord, bring me low;
For Thou wert lowly in Thy blessed heart:
Lord, keep me so.
Amen.

—CHRISTINA ROSSETTI (1830–1894)

Evening

Merciful Lord, of Thy abundant goodness towards us
Thou hast made the day wherein to work,
and ordained the night wherein to take our rest;
grant us such rest of body, that we may have a waking soul.
Let no vain and wandering fancy trouble us;
let our spiritual enemies have no power over us,
but let our minds be set wholly upon Thy presence,
to love, and fear, and rest in Thee alone,
that being refreshed with moderate and sober sleep,
we may rise up again, with cheerful strength and gladness,
to serve Thee in all good works;
through Jesus Christ our Lord.
Amen.

—JOHN COSIN (1594–1672)

Morning

The day returns and brings me the petty round
of irritating concerns and duties. . . .
Help me to perform them with laughter and kind face,
let cheerfulness abound with industry.
Give me to go blithely on my business all this day;
bring me to my resting bed weary and content and undishonored;
and grant me in the end the gift of sleep.
Amen.

—ROBERT LOUIS STEVENSON (1850–1894)

Evening

May God the Father bless me;
Jesus Christ, defend and keep me;
the power of the Holy Spirit, enlighten me and sanctify me
this night and forever.
Amen.

—*A MANUAL OF DEVOTION* (1876)

Morning

Be Thou my vision, O Lord of my heart;
Naught be all else to me, save that Thou art:
Thou my best thought by day or by night,
Waking or sleeping, Thy presence my light. . . .

Riches I heed not, nor man's empty praise,
Thou mine inheritance, now and always:
Thou and Thou only first in my heart,
High King of heaven, my treasure Thou art.

High King of heaven, my victory won
May I reach heaven's joys, O bright heaven's Son!
Heart of my own heart, whatever befall,
Still be my vision, O Ruler of all.
Amen.

—ANCIENT IRISH PRAYER (c. 6TH c.);
TRANSLATED BY MARY BYRNE (1880–1931)

Evening

Lighten our darkness, we beseech Thee, O Lord;
and by Your great mercy defend us from all perils
and dangers of this night;
for the love of Your only Son,
our Savior, Jesus Christ.
Amen.

—GELASIAN SACRAMENTARY (8TH c.)

Morning

Maker of the Morning,
as the blazing sun glories the eastern horizon,
I arise and greet this new day.
My spirit bows with gratitude,
rejoicing in hope for what this day promises. . . .
As people of the sleepy earth stretch and stir,
awaken in them an eagerness for Your wisdom. . . .
May this day be a day of peace for all of creation,
with Your touch of compassion extended to each one.
I commit all that awakens in my heart
into the gracious hands of Your care.
I dedicate all I am and all I do this day to You,
the Radiant One of the morning.
I entrust my entire being into the protective arms of Your love.
Amen.

—JOYCE RUPP (1943–)

Evening

I will both lie down in peace, and sleep;
For You alone, O LORD, make me dwell in safety.
Amen.

—PSALM 4:8

Morning

Make my body healthy and agile,
my mind sharp and clear,
my heart joyful and contented,
my soul faithful and loving. . . .
Above all let me live in Your presence,
for with You all fear is banished,
and there is only harmony and peace.
Let every day combine the beauty of spring,
the brightness of summer,
the abundance of autumn,
and the repose of winter.
And at the end of my life on earth,
grant that I may come to see and know You in the fullness of your glory.
Amen.

—THOMAS AQUINAS (1225–1274)

Evening

As the evening shadows fall,
closing out the light of the day,
come, merciful Savior, with Your benedictions into my heart.
Bring to me the full forgiveness of all my sins
and grant me Your glorious peace which passes all understanding.
Relax my body and give me much-needed rest.
Amen.

—*MY PRAYER BOOK* (1980)

Morning

Glory be to You, O Lord, my Creator.
Glory be to You, Jesus, my Redeemer.
Glory be to You, Holy Spirit, my Sanctifier, Guide and Comforter.
All love, all glory, be to the high and undivided Trinity,
whose deeds are inseparable, and whose worldwide rule is forever;
to You, and to You alone, and to Your Son, and to the Holy Spirit,
be glory forever and ever!
Amen.

—THOMAS WILSON (1663–1755)

Evening

Remember Your mercies, Lord.
In Your love remember me.
Let Your peace rest upon me.
Enfold me in Your everlasting love.
Hold me close to Your heart, O Lord.
God bless all those I love.
God bless all those that love me.
God bless all those that love those that I love,
and all those that love those that love me.
Amen.

—FROM AN OLD NEW ENGLAND SAMPLER

Morning

Wherever I am, whatever I do, Thou,
Lord, seest me:
O, keep me in Thy fear all day long.
Lord, give me grace to keep always a conscience void of offence
towards Thee and towards men.
Lord, teach me so to number my days,
that I may apply my heart to wisdom.
O, let my mouth be filled with Thy praise,
that I may sing of Thy glory and honour all the day long.
Amen.

—Bishop Thomas Ken (1637–1711)

Evening

O gladsome Light of the holy glory of the Immortal Father,
heavenly, holy, blessed Jesus Christ!
Now that I have come to the setting of the sun
and behold the light of evening,
I praise Thee: Father, Son, and Holy Spirit.
For meet it is at all times to worship Thee with voices of praise,
O Son of God, and Giver of Life.
Therefore all the world glorifies You.
Amen.

—Eastern Orthodox hymn at Office of Vespers (2nd c.)

Morning

Lord, help me to glorify Thee. . . .
Help me to glorify Thee by contentment. . . .
I have talents, help me to extol Thee by spending them for Thee.
I have time, Lord, help me to redeem it, that I may serve Thee.
I have a heart to feel, Lord, let that heart feel no love but Thine. . . .
I have a head to think, Lord, help me to think of Thee and for Thee.
Thou hast put me in this world for something, Lord;
show me what that is, and help me to work out my life-purpose.
Amen.

—CHARLES SPURGEON (1834–1892)

Evening

O Lord, You have measured the heights and the earth
in the hollow of Your hand,
and created the six-winged Seraphim to cry out to You
with an unceasing voice:
"Holy, Holy, Holy, glory to Your name."
Deliver me from the mouth of the evil one, O Master.
Forget my many evil deeds
and through the multitude of Your compassions,
grant me daily forgiveness, for You are blessed unto the ages.
Amen.

—SARRAH (4TH C.)

Morning

O Creator God,
both the thick darkness of the night
and the gleaming light of the day
are gifts from You.
Thank You for the darkness:
for rest, forgetfulness, blessed silence.
Thank You for the light:
for action, purpose, blessed voices.
The night and the day come from You—
this day I dedicate to You,
through Christ my Lord.
Amen.

—DAVID P. GUSHEE (1962–)

Evening

Now the light goes away.
Savior, listen while I pray,
Asking Thee to watch and keep,
And to send me quiet sleep.
Jesus, Savior, wash away
All that has been wrong today.
Help me everyday to be
Good and gentle, more like Thee. . . .
Now my evening praise I give:
Thou didst die that I might live;
All my blessings come from Thee;
Oh how good Thou art to me!
Amen.

—FRANCES RIDLEY HAVERGAL (1836–1879)

Morning

O my God, deep calls unto deep. . . . only You can give that solid assurance
and the support that I need. There can be no existence without You.
I find that there is only one reality, and that is that You are always dependable.
I look to find what my heart can love; and it is only Love.
I look up and down the streets of the city, and throughout the countryside.
But I find that they who live to themselves,
are strangers from the life before God.
I search everywhere, in all the wide realms of the world,
in all that is inside me, as well as all that is outside me,
including all the crises of my life,
but they only highlight the reality that I need You.
They also attest the truth that the kingdom of God is within me.
For I find You in my heart. . . .
Amen.

—WILLIAM OF ST. THIERRY (c. 1085–1148)

Evening

The desire of all my soul: Your name;
the desire of my soul: the thought of You.
Preferences, tastes, wishes—
these bubble up, flicker out
in the moment's unthinking rejoinders;
but the desire of my soul is for You.
My soul desires You at night;
my spirit seeks You within me.
Always, everywhere
the silver thread firm in a maze of color,
the theme unchanged through weaving variations,
the desire of my soul is for You.
Amen.

—ANONYMOUS (15TH c.), BASED ON ISAIAH 26:8–9

Morning

O everlasting God,
who hast ordained . . . the ministries of angels and men
in a wonderful order:
mercifully grant that, as Thy holy angels always serve
and worship Thee in heaven,
so by Thy appointment they may help and defend us on earth;
through Jesus Christ our Lord . . .
Amen.

—BOOK OF COMMON PRAYER (1979)

Evening

O Christ, Son of the Living God,
May Your holy angels guard our sleep.
May they watch over us as we rest
And hover around our beds. . . .
May no dreams disturb our rest
And no nightmares darken our dreams. . . .
May the virtue of our daily work
Hallow our nightly prayers.
May our sleep be deep and soft,
So our work be fresh and hard.
Amen.

—PATRICK OF IRELAND (c. 387–c. 460)

Morning

My God, Father and Preserver,
who in Your goodness has watched over me
in this past night and brought me to this day,
grant that I may spend the day
wholly in Your service.
Let me not think or say or do
a single thing that is not in obedience to Your will;
but rather let all my actions
be directed to Your glory
and the salvation of my brethren.
Let me attempt nothing that is not pleasing to You . . .
Grant also, that as I labour
for the goods and clothing necessary for this life,
I may constantly raise my mind
upwards to the heavenly life
which You promise to all Your children.
Amen.

—JOHN CALVIN (1509–1564)

Evening

Calm me, O Lord, as You stilled the storm;
Still me, O Lord; keep me from harm.
Let all the storms within me cease.
Enfold me, Lord, in Your peace.
Amen.

—CELTIC PRAYER

October 1

Loving and tender providence of my God,
into Your hands I commend my spirit;
to You I abandon my hopes and fears,
my desires and repugnances,
my temporal and eternal prospects.
To You I commit the wants of my perishable body;
to You I commit the more precious interests of my immortal soul
for whose lot I have nothing to fear
as long as I do not leave Your care.
Though my faults are many . . .
my spiritual poverty extreme,
my hope in You surpasses all.
It is superior to my weakness,
greater than my difficulties,
stronger than death.
Though temptations should assail me,
I will hope in You. . . .
You are my kind, compassionate, and indulgent parent,
and I am Your devoted child
who casts myself into Your arms and begs Your blessing.
Amen.

—Claude La Colombière (1641–1682)

Evening

Holy Lord, almighty and eternal Father,
thank You for Your mercy that has protected me throughout this day.
Let me pass through this night peacefully
and with a pure mind and body,
that rising with purity in the morning,
I may serve You gratefully.
Amen.

—Alcuin of York (c. 735–804)

OCTOBER 2

Morning

Grant me, I beseech Thee, O Lord,
grace to follow Thee wheresoever Thou goest.
In little daily duties to which Thou callest me,
bow down my will to simple obedience,
patience under pain or provocation,
strict truthfulness in word or manner, humility and kindness.
In great acts of duty or perfection,
if Thou shouldest call me to them,
uplift me to sacrifice and heroic courage;
that in all things, both small and great,
I may be an imitator of Thy dear Son,
even Jesus Christ our Lord.
Amen.

—Christina Rossetti (1830–1894)

Evening

I humbly beg of You, God the Father almighty,
to bless and sanctify our home,
those who live in it and everything in it.
Be so kind as to fill it with all good things.
Grant us, Lord, abundance of blessings from heaven
and the substance of life from the richness of the earth.
Direct the longings of our prayers to the fruits of Your mercy.
Be so kind, then, as to bless and sanctify this home at our coming in . . .
May Your angels of light live within the walls of this house,
and guard it and all who live in it, through Christ our Lord.
Amen.

—Catholic prayer

OCTOBER 3

Morning

O God, who hast so greatly loved us,
long sought us,
and mercifully redeemed us,
give us grace that in everything we may yield ourselves,
our wills and our works,
a continual thank-offering to You;
through Jesus Christ our Lord.
Amen.

—Westminster Confession of Faith (1647)

Evening

Do Thou, O Lord God, whom we worship,
O Holy King Jesus Christ,
keep me while I sleep by Thy unfading light, Thy Holy Spirit,
with which Thou didst hallow Thy disciples.
O Lord, grant even to me, Thy unworthy servant,
Thy salvation on my bed:
enlighten my mind with the light
of the understanding of Thy holy Gospel,
my soul with the love of Thy Cross,
my heart with the purity of Thy Word,
my body with Thy passionless passion.
Keep my thought in Thy humility,
and rouse me in due time to glorify Thee.
For Thou art most glorified,
together with Thine Eternal Father
and the Most Holy Spirit unto the ages.
Amen.

—Antiochus (d. 410)

Morning

Lord, make me an instrument of Thy peace.
Where there is hatred, let me sow love;
where there is injury, pardon.
Where there is discord, vision.
Where there is doubt, faith.
Where there is despair, hope.
Where there is darkness, light.
Where there is sadness, joy.
O Divine Master, grant that I may not so much seek
to be consoled as to console;
to be understood as to understand;
to be loved, as to love;
for it is in giving that we receive,
it is in pardoning that we are pardoned,
and it is in dying that we are born to eternal life.
Amen.

—FRANCIS OF ASSISI (1181–1226)

Evening

Lord Jesus Christ,
who are called the Prince of Peace, who are Yourself
our peace and reconciliation,
who so often said, "Peace to you," grant us peace.
Make all men and women witnesses of truth, justice, and brotherly love.
Banish from their hearts whatever might endanger peace.
Enlighten our rulers that they may guarantee
and defend the great gift of peace.
May all peoples on the earth become as brothers and sisters.
May longed for peace blossom forth and reign always over us all.
Amen.

—POPE JOHN XXIII (1881–1963)

October 5

Morning

O God,
who brought me from the rest of last night
unto the joyous light of this day,
bring me from the new light of this day
unto the guiding light of eternity.
Amen.

—*Carmina Gadelica* (1900)

Evening

I thank Thee, Lord God and Father, Creator of heaven and earth,
for all Thy good gifts which I, O Father of lights, have received of Thee,
and receive daily of Thy liberal hand through Jesus Christ,
the dearly beloved Son, our Lord,
Thou who hast clothed my body with the needed covering
and hast satisfied it with the natural bread.
I pray Thee humbly, as my dearly beloved Father,
to look upon me, Thy child, . . .
earnestly desirous, in my weakness, to live devoutly in this world.
Be pleased to keep me in Thy Word in fatherly fashion,
in order that to the end of my days I may remain constant
in Thy Word and Gospel.
Amen.

—Menno Simons (c. 1496–1561)

OCTOBER 6

Morning

O Lord, take full possession of my heart, raise there Your throne,
and command there as You do in heaven.
Being created by You, let me live for You;
being created for You, let me always act for Your glory;
being redeemed by You, let me give to You what is Yours;
and let my spirit cling to You alone, for Your name's sake.
Amen.

—JOHN WESLEY (1703–1791)

Evening

My God,
I love You with all my heart.
I thank You for having kept me safe this day.
Pardon me the evil I have done, and accept the good I have done.
Take care of me while I sleep and deliver me from all danger.
May Your grace be always with me and with my loved ones.
Amen.

—ANONYMOUS CATHOLIC PRAYER

OCTOBER 7

Morning

O Thou, who art from everlasting to everlasting,
without beginning or ending of days,
replenish me with heavenly grace at the beginning of this day,
that I may be enabled to accept all its duties,
to perform all its labors, to welcome all its mercies,
to meet all its trials,
and to advance through all it holds in store for me
with cheerful courage and a constant mind.
Amen.

—BOOK OF COMMON PRAYER (1928)

Evening

Peace be unto this home.
And unto all who dwell herein. . . .
Be merciful to me, O God,
for great is Thy goodness. . . .
And deign to send Thy holy angel
from heaven to guard, cherish,
protect, visit, and defend
all who dwell in this home.
Through Christ our Lord.
Amen.

—CATHOLIC BLESSING

OCTOBER 8

I bind unto myself today
The power of God to hold and lead,
His eye to watch,
His might to stay,
His ear to hearken to my need,
The wisdom of my God to teach,
His hand to guide, His shield to ward,
The Word of God to give me speech,
His heavenly host to be my guard.
Amen.

—PATRICK OF IRELAND (c. 387–c. 460)

Evening

Lord, the only God. . . .
You are beauty,
You are gentleness.
You are our protector,
You are our guardian and defender.
You are our courage,
You are our haven and our hope.
You are our faith, our great consolation.
You are our eternal life,
great and wonderful Lord,
God almighty, merciful Saviour.
Amen.

—FRANCIS OF ASSISI (1181–1226)

Morning

Lord, strengthen my faith that it be not dead and ineffectual,
but lively, showing itself in good works
and conforming ever more closely
to the image of Christ in whom we believe.
I ask this through that same Christ Jesus our Lord.
Amen.

—Dean Addison (1605)

Evening

Now we must praise
the Guardian of the kingdom of heaven,
the might of the Creator,
and His wisdom,
the work of the Father of Glory;
for He, the Eternal Lord,
appointed each wondrous thing
from the beginning.
He, the Holy Creator,
first made heaven as a roof
for the children of men.
And afterward He,
the Guardian of mankind,
the Eternal Lord,
the Almighty Master,
fashioned the earth for mortals.
Amen.

—Caedmon (d. 684)

October 10

Morning

O Lord God, I humbly beseech Thee to direct
my thoughts and prayers this day;
purify my heart from every evil and false imagination,
and may no vain and worldly desires have their abode in me.
Keep me from all wandering looks and ways,
from an undevout mind, and careless prayers.
Let the voice of Thy love enter my soul,
that I may study Thy word with reverence and holy fear,
with fervor and delight.
O God, Thou seest me: help me to look up unto Thee;
for the sake of Thy Son, Jesus Christ, our Lord.
Amen.

—*The Offices for Special Occasions* (1916)

Evening

Lord,
You have been with me all through this day, stay with me now.
As the shadows lengthen into darkness let the noisy world grow quiet,
let its feverish concerns be stilled, its voices silenced.
In the final moments of this day remind me of what is real.
But let me not forget that You were as present in
the stresses of the day just past as You are now in the silence of this night.
You have made me for day and for night, for work and for rest . . .
Here in this night let me embrace and not regret
the mysterious beauty of my humanity.
Keep me in the embrace of Your reality through the night,
and the day to come.
Surround me with Your silence and give me the rest
that only You can give—
real peace, now and forever.
Amen.

—Evelyn Underhill (1875–1941),
adapted by John Kirvan (1932–2012)

Morning

Lord of the morning, and Ruler of all seasons,
hear my prayer and have mercy on my soul.
Shine upon me, Lord, and I shall be light like the day;
I will sing Your praise in light while I marvel;
may the morning awaken me to the praise of Your Godhead
and I will pursue the study of Your Word all of the day. . . .
The morning and the evening shall praise You, Lord,
in their changes, and will present You the sweet incense
of their offering.
Amen.

—Syrian Orthodox prayer

Evening

O God, Creator of all things, and Ruler of the heavens,
it is Thou that clothest day with beautiful light,
and night with the boon of sleep.
It is sleep that restores our wearied limbs to the toil of work.
Sleep gives repose to the mind when tired,
and takes away the anxious-making grief.
The day is spent, and night is come;
I offer Thee my thanks and prayers. . . .
May my heart's deepest self,
unshackled by the allurements of the senses, dream of Thee;
do not let the fear of the enemy,
whose envy is ever laying snares, disturb me when at rest.
Let my prayer ascend to Christ, and to the Father,
and to the Spirit of Christ and Father:
O Trinity, one in essence and all-powerful,
be merciful to me, who pray to Thee.
Amen.

—Ambrose of Milan (339–397)

OCTOBER 12

Morning

Teach me, Lord, to be sweet and gentle in the events of life,
in disappointments, in the thoughtlessness of others.
Let me put myself aside, to think of the happiness of others.
Teach me to profit by the suffering that comes across my path;
let me use it that it may mellow me, not harden and embitter me,
that it may make me patient, not irritable,
that it may make me broad in my forgiveness. . . .
May no one be less good for having come within my influence;
no one less pure, less true, less kind, less noble
for having been a fellow traveler in our journey toward eternal life.
As I go my rounds from one distraction to another,
let me whisper, from time to time, a word of love to You.
May my life be lived in the supernatural, full of power for good,
and strong in its purpose of sanctity.
Dear Jesus, help me to spread Your fragrance everywhere.
Flood my soul with Your Spirit and life.
Penetrate and possess my whole being so completely
that my life may be only a radiance of Yours.
Shine through me and be so in me
that every soul I come in contact with may feel Your presence in my soul.
Amen.

—CARDINAL JOHN HENRY NEWMAN (1801–1890)

Evening

Thou that has given so much to me,
Give one thing more, a grateful heart.
Not thankful when it pleases me,
As if Thy blessings had spare days;
But such a heart whose very pulse
May be Thy praise.
Amen.

—GEORGE HERBERT (1593–1633)

Morning

Jesus,
help me to simplify my life by learning what
You want me to be
and becoming that person.
Amen.

—THÉRÈSE OF LISIEUX (1873–1897)

Evening

Assistant of workers,
Benefactor of the good,
Custodian on the ramparts,
Defender of the faithful,
Exalter of the humble,
Frustrator of the proud,
Governor of the faithful.
Hostile to the impenitent,
Judge of all judges,
Light and Father of lights,
Magnificent shining light,
Never denying to the hopeful,
Offering help to the needful.
Poor am I, a little person,
Quaking and wretched,
Rowing through the storm,
Sacredly drawing to Heaven,
Towards the supernal Haven, I come through You, Christ Jesus.
Vital, most beautiful gate, is Christ; angels sing,
Yielding praise eternally to the
Zenith, proof against foes.
Amen.

—*ADIUTOR LABORANTIUM*, PRAYER FROM IONA MONASTERY (7TH C.)

OCTOBER 14

Morning

O let me hear Thy loving-kindness in the morning,
for in Thee is my trust.
Teach me to do the thing that pleaseth Thee,
for Thou art my God.
Let Thy loving Spirit lead me forth
into the land of righteousness.
Amen.

—LANCELOT ANDREWES (1555–1626)

Evening

Be with us, Lord Jesus, tonight.
Stay to adore and praise the Father,
and give thanks to the Father for us while we sleep;
to draw down mercy and grace upon the world. . . .
Stay with us, to guard the innocent,
to sustain the tempted, to raise the fallen,
to curb the power of the evil one, to prevent sin.
Stay with us, to comfort the sorrowing. . . .
O Good Shepherd, stay with Your sheep.
Secure them against the perils that beset them.
Stay, above all, with the suffering and dying.
Grant us a quiet night and a perfect end.
Be our merciful Shepherd to the last,
that without fear we may appear
before You as our Judge.
Amen.

—CATHOLIC PRAYER (19TH C.)

OCTOBER 15

Morning

Almighty, eternal and merciful God,
whose word is a lamp unto my feet
and a light unto my path,
open and illuminate my mind,
that I may purely and perfectly understand Thy Word,
and that my life may be conformed
to what I have rightly understood,
that in nothing I may be displeasing unto Thy majesty,
through Jesus Christ our Lord.
Amen.

—Ulrich Zwingli (1484–1531)

Evening

O my God! Who would not love You?
O good Jesus! When will I begin to love You
as I am obliged?
How far am I from this perfect, intimate and generous love!
Alas, I know not even how to love You . . .
What advantage is it to have a heart,
unless it be quite consumed with love for You!
Amen.

—Rose of Lima (1586–1617)

Morning

Behold, Lord, an empty vessel
that needs to be filled.
My Lord, fill it.
I am weak in the faith;
strengthen me.
I am cold in love;
warm me and make me fervent
that my love may go out to my neighbor.
I do not have a strong and firm faith;
at times I doubt
and am unable to trust You altogether.
O Lord, help me.
Amen.

—MARTIN LUTHER (1483–1546)

Evening

Into Your hands, O Lord,
I commend my spirit this night,
for You have redeemed me, O Lord,
O God of goodness and truth.
Keep me, O Lord, as the apple of Your eye;
hide me under the shadow of Your wings.
Amen.

—BOOK OF COMMON PRAYER (1928)

October 17

Morning

Give us, O Lord, we humbly beseech Thee,
a wise, a sober, a patient understanding, a courageous heart;
a soul full of devotion to do Thee service,
and strength against all temptations,
through Jesus Christ our Lord.
Amen.

—Archbishop William Laud (1573–1645)

Evening

Dear Holy Spirit,
You are my friend.
I give You myself.
I ask You to dwell deeply inside of me
and make me holy.
I want to know the fire of God's love.
I want to love God with all my heart.
Amen.

—Catholic prayer

OCTOBER 18

Morning

I ask for Your help, Father of Christ,
Lord of all that is, Creator of all the created, Maker of all that is made;
I stretch out clean hands to You and lay bare my mind, Lord, before You.
Have mercy, I pray You; spare me, be kind to me, improve me;
fill me with virtue, faith and knowledge.
Look at me, Lord; I bring my weakness for You to see.
Be kind and merciful to me . . .
make me equitable, temperate, and pure;
send out angelic powers to make me . . . holy and noble.
Send the Holy Spirit into my mind, I beg You,
and grant that I may learn to understand
the holy scriptures He inspired. . . .
Through Your only Son Jesus Christ, in the Holy Spirit.
Through Him may glory and power be Yours, now and age after age.
Amen.

—SERAPION (D. 360)

Evening

Oh! Bring me, I pray You, now near to Yourself.
Let me bathe myself in communion with my God.
Blessed be the love which chose me before the world began!
I can never sufficiently adore You for Your sovereignty,
the sovereignty of love which saw us in the ruins of the Fall,
yet loved us anyway. . . .
And now to Father, Son, and Holy Spirit be glory forever and ever.
Amen.

—CHARLES SPURGEON (1834–1892)

OCTOBER 19

Morning

My heart I give you, Lord, eagerly and entirely.
Amen.

—John Calvin (1509–1564)

Evening

Here I am, Lord Spirit,
watching Your sun setting down,
watching for Your peace to settle down in me.
The sky is going yellow,
white, and mauve, and the
air is cool but still.
Another day of Yours is quietly burning out.
A homing dove is wheeling circles restfully,
while commence around me
the whirring, murmuring lullabies of night.
I did not live this day in gratitude.
I believe that it will come.

How busy before Your throne we make ourselves
in this drive-and-buy-it, hub-bub, paltry age!

But not me, now.
The earth and I are taut
with hushed expectancy of dark.
All strivings of mine are quietly burning out.
The knack of faith is being emptied, trustfully;
only the empty can be filled.
As the nest waits
for the bird to fly home,
so wait I for Your rest.
Amen.

—Jeanie Gushee (1962–)

October 20

Morning

In the silence of the early morning
Your Spirit hovers over the brink of the day
and new light pierces the darkness of the night.
In the silence of the morning
life begins to stir around me
and I listen for the day's first utterances.
In earth, sea and sky
and in the landscape of my own soul
I listen for utterances of Your love, O God.
I listen for utterances of Your love.
Amen.

—J. Philip Newell (1953—)

Evening

O my God, I firmly believe that Thou art here present,
and plainly seest me, and that Thou deservest
all my actions, all my thoughts,
and the most secret motions of my heart.
Thou watchest over me with an incomparable love,
every moment bestowing favors,
and preserving me from evil.
Blessed be Thy holy name,
and may all creatures bless Thy goodness
for the benefits which I have ever received from Thee, and
particularly this day.
May the saints and angels supply my defect
in rendering Thee due thanks.
Never permit me to be so base and wicked
as to repay Thy bounties with ingratitude.
Amen.

—*Catholic Prayer Book* (1866)

October 21

Morning

Direct me, O Lord,
in all my doings with Thy most gracious favor,
and further me with Thy continual help;
that in all my works begun, continued, and ended in Thee,
I may glorify Thy holy Name,
and finally, by Thy mercy, obtain everlasting life;
through Jesus Christ our Lord.
Amen.

—BOOK OF COMMON PRAYER (1979)

Evening

My Lord and my God,
take me from all that keeps me from You.
My Lord and my God,
grant me all that leads me to You.
My Lord and my God,
take me from myself and give me completely to You.
Amen.

—NICHOLAS OF FLUE (1417–1487)

OCTOBER 22

Morning

Ah, cement me to Thee, O true Love!
I offer Thee my love because Thou art altogether dulcet and pleasant,
my Lord, full of delight.
I vow obedience to Thee because Thy fatherly charity allures me,
Thy loving kindness and gentleness attract me.
In observing Thy will, I tie myself to Thee,
because clinging to Thee is lovable above everything.
Amen.

—GERTRUDE THE GREAT (1256–c. 1302)

Evening

Helper of men who turn to You,
Light of men in the dark,
Creator of all that grows from seed,
Promoter of all spiritual growth,
have mercy, Lord, on me
and make me a temple fit for Yourself.
Do not scan my transgressions too closely,
for if You are quick to notice my offenses,
I shall not dare to appear before You.
In Your great mercy,
in Your boundless compassion,
wash away my sins, through Jesus Christ,
Your only Child, the truly holy,
the chief of our souls' healers.
Through Him may all glory be given You,
all power and honor and praise,
throughout the unending succession of ages.
Amen.

—PRAYER FROM EGYPT (4TH c.)

Morning

O Lord Jesus Christ,
who when on earth wast ever occupied about Thy Father's business:
grant that I may not grow weary in well-doing.
Give me grace to do all in Thy Name;
be Thou the beginning and the end of all;
the pattern whom I follow,
the Redeemer in whom I trust,
the Master whom I serve,
the Friend to whom I look for sympathy.
May I never shrink from my duty through any fear of man;
make me faithful unto death;
and bring me at last into Thy eternal Presence,
where with the Father and the Holy Ghost,
Thou livest and reignest for ever.
Amen.

—EDWARD BOUVERIE PUSEY (1800–1882)

Evening

O Father,
come and rest Your children now.
Take the helmet from our brow,
remove from us the weight
of our heavy armor for a while,
and may we just have peace,
perfect peace,
and be at rest.
Amen.

—CHARLES SPURGEON (1834–1892)

OCTOBER 24

Morning

O Lord God, destroy and root out whatever the adversary plants in me,
that with my sins destroyed You may sow understanding
and good work in my mouth and heart;
so that in act and in truth I may serve only You
and know how to fulfill the commandments of Christ and to see Yourself.
Give me love, give me chastity, give me faith,
give me all things which You know belong to the profit of my soul.
O Lord, work good in me,
and provide me with what You know that I need.
Amen.

—COLUMBANUS (c. 550–615)

Evening

You alone are unutterable,
from the time You created all things that can be spoken of. . . .
All things cry out about You;
those which speak, and those which cannot speak.
All things honour You;
those which think, and those which cannot think.
For there is one longing, one groaning,
that all things have for You. . . .
All things pray to You that comprehend Your plan
and offer You a silent hymn.
In You, the One, all things abide,
and all things endlessly run to You
who are the end of all.
Amen.

—GREGORY OF NAZIANZUS (c. 325–389)

OCTOBER 25

Morning

O Jesus . . . come and live in Thy servant,
in the spirit of Thy sanctity,
in the fullness of Thy strength,
in the reality of Thy virtues,
in the perfection of Thy ways,
in the communion of Thy mysteries,
be Lord over every opposing power,
in Thine own Spirit, to the glory of the Father.
Amen.

—JEAN-JACQUES OLIER (1608–1657)

Evening

O Holy Spirit, most merciful Comforter:
You proceed from the Father in a manner beyond our understanding.
Come, I beseech You, and take up Your abode in my heart.
Purify and cleanse me from all sin, and sanctify my soul.
Cleanse it from every impurity, water its dryness, melt its coldness,
and save it from sinful ways.
Make me truly humble and resigned, that I may be pleasing to You,
and that You abide with me forever.
Most blessed Light, most amiable Light, enlighten me. . . .
My God, give Yourself to me,
and kindle in my innermost soul the fire of Your love.
My Lord, please instruct, direct, and defend me in all things.
Give me strength against all immoderate fears
and against despondency.
Bestow upon me a true faith, a firm hope,
and a sincere and perfect love.
Grant that I always do Your most gracious will.
Amen.

—ANTIOCHUS (D. 410)

Morning

Eternal God,
the light of the minds that know You,
the life of the souls that love You,
the strength of the wills that serve You;
help me so to know You that I may truly love You,
so to love You that I may fully serve You,
whom to serve is perfect freedom.
Amen.

—AUGUSTINE OF HIPPO (354–430)

Evening

Make it my delight O God
to do Thy will,
and let Thy law be written in my heart. . . .
May I take unto me the whole armour of God,
and resist the devil,
and overcome the world,
and be more than conqueror through Christ that hath loved us;
that having fought the good fight of faith,
I may lay hold on eternal life;
and blessed and heavenly Father,
for all Thy abounding mercies and blessings vouchsafed to me. . . .
I desire to render praise, honour, renown and thanksgiving
to Thy great and excellent name, for Thou alone art worthy,
who art God over all,
blessed for ever and ever.
Amen.

—WILLIAM PENN (1644–1718)

Morning

O Lord,
give me that due sense
of all Thy mercies,
that my heart may be
unfeignedly thankful, and that I show forth
Thy praise, not only with
my lips, but in my life,
by giving up myself to Thy
service, and by walking
before Thee in holiness
and righteousness all my days;
through Jesus Christ my
Lord, to whom, with Thee
and the Holy Ghost,
be all honour and glory, world without end.
Amen.

—BOOK OF COMMON PRAYER (1662)

Evening

I turn my thoughts quietly, O God, away from self to Thee.
I adore Thee. I praise Thee. I thank Thee.
I here turn from this feverish life to think of Thy holiness—
Thy love—Thy serenity—Thy joy—
Thy mighty purposefulness—Thy wisdom—Thy beauty—
Thy truth—Thy final omnipotence.
Amen.

—LESLIE WEATHERHEAD (1893–1976)

Morning

You are Wisdom. . . .
Raise me, I pray, that I may wholly respond to . . .
Your words, mysterious and inspired.
There all God's secret matters lie covered and hidden under darkness
both profound and brilliant, silent and wise.
You make what is ultimate and beyond brightness secretly to shine
in all that is most dark.
In Your way, ever unseen and intangible,
You fill to the full with most beautiful splendor
those souls who close their eyes that they may see.
And I, please, with love that goes on beyond mind
to All that is beyond mind,
seek to gain such for myself through prayer.
Amen.

—*The Cloud of Unknowing* (14th c.)

Evening

Now God be with us for the night is closing;
The light and darkness are of His disposing;
And 'neath His shadow here to rest we yield us,
For He will shield us.
Let evil thoughts and spirits flee before us;
Till morning cometh, watch, O Master o'er us;
In soul and body Thou from harm defend us,
Thine angels send us.
Amen.

—Petrus Herbert (1533–1571); translated by
Catherine Winkworth (1827–1878)

October 29

Morning

Almighty God, whose glory the heavens are telling,
the earth Thy power and the sea Thy might,
and whose greatness all feeling creatures everywhere herald:
to Thee belongeth glory, honour, might,
greatness and magnificence,
now and for ever,
to the ages of ages.
Amen.

—Liturgy of St. James (4th c.)

Evening

Give me an upright heart which no unworthy purpose may tempt aside.
Bestow upon me also, O Lord my God, understanding to know Thee,
diligence to seek Thee,
wisdom to find Thee,
and a faithfulness that may finally embrace Thee;
through Jesus Christ our Lord.
Amen.

—Thomas Aquinas (1225–1274)

October 30

Morning

Lord God,
You are holy, surpassing human expression:
You made light shine out of darkness,
and in our night's sleep have given us rest . . .
Make us children of the light,
inheritors of Your eternal goodness . . .
For You are the God of compassion,
full of goodness and love for all mankind,
and we give You glory,
Father, Son and Holy Spirit,
now and for ever,
to the ages of ages.
Amen.

—EASTERN ORTHODOX PRAYER

Evening

I will extol You, my God, O King;
And I will bless Your name forever and ever.
Every day I will bless You,
And I will praise Your name forever and ever.
Great is the LORD, and greatly to be praised;
And His greatness is unsearchable.
Amen.

—PSALM 145:1–3

Morning

To Thee,
O Master that lovest all men,
I hasten on rising from sleep;
by Thy mercy I go forth to do Thy work, and I pray to Thee:
help me at all times, in everything;
deliver me from every evil thing of this world
and from every attack of the devil;
save me and bring me into Thine eternal Kingdom.
For Thou art my Creator, the Giver and Provider of everything good;
in Thee is all my hope, and to Thee I ascribe glory,
now and ever, and to the ages of ages.
Amen.

—MACARIUS OF EGYPT (c. 300–390)

Evening

From ghoulies and ghosties
and long-leggity beasties,
and all things that go bump in the night,
Good Lord, deliver us!
Amen.

—TRADITIONAL SCOTTISH PRAYER

THE APOSTLE PAUL

November 1: All Saints' Day

Morning

How shining and splendid are Your gifts, O Lord,
which You give us for our eternal well-being!
Your glory shines radiantly in Your saints, O God,
in the honour and the noble victory of the martyrs.
The white-robed company follow You, bright with their abundant faith;
they scorned the wicked words of those with this world's power.
For You they sustained fierce beatings, chains, and torments;
they were drained by cruel punishments;
they bore their holy witness to You,
who were grounded deep within their hearts;
they were sustained by patience and constancy.
Endowed with Your everlasting grace,
may we rejoice for ever with the martyrs in our bright fatherland.
O Christ, in Your goodness, grant to us
the gracious heavenly realms of eternal life.
Amen.

—Anonymous (10th c.)

Evening

The glorious choir of the apostles praise Thee.
The admirable company of the prophets praise Thee.
The white-robed army of martyrs praise Thee.
The holy church throughout the world doth acknowledge Thee,
the Father of infinite majesty, Thy venerable true and only Son,
and the Holy Spirit the Comforter. . . .
We beseech Thee, therefore, help Thy servants,
whom Thou hast redeemed with Thy precious blood.
Make them to be numbered with Thy saints in glory everlasting.
Amen.

—All Saints Antiphon at Lauds, from *Te Deum* (4th c.)

November 2

Morning

I give You thanks,
our God and Father,
for all those who have died in the faith of Christ;
for the memory of their words and deeds
and all they accomplished in their time;
for the joyful hope of reunion with them in the world to come;
and for our communion with them now
in Your Son, Jesus Christ our Lord.
Amen.

—Anonymous

Evening

May the souls of the faithful departed,
through the mercy of God, rest in peace.
Amen.

—The Treasury of Devotion (1876)

Morning

Glory to You,
Christ our God, our hope, glory to You!
Heavenly King, Comforter, the Spirit of Truth,
present in all places and filling all things,
Treasury of goodness and Giver of light and life:
come and abide in us.
Cleanse us from every stain of sin and save our souls,
O gracious Lord.
Amen.

—EASTERN ORTHODOX PRAYER

Evening

Lord,
go with each of us to rest;
if any awake, temper to them
the dark hours of watching;
and when the day returns,
return to us, our sun and comforter.
Amen.

—ROBERT LOUIS STEVENSON (1850–1894)

NOVEMBER 4

Morning

This morning my soul is greater than the world
since it possesses You,
You whom heaven and earth do not contain.
Amen.

—MARGARET OF CORTONA (1247–1297)

Evening

For starshine, Sir, in a long night,
each glistening of a giving light;
for rocking chairs with glides gentle,
similar to Your parental
rotating earth from dark to bright;
for small, wild creatures who crouch
in dens, as I, as wild, do couch
in mine; for birds' drowsy twitters,
mums, grans, babysitters,
and all who murmur in the night
hushed and lovely lullabies
to lull and close an infant's eyes
(sparkly as stars in midnight gaze!),
an evensong, Good Sir, I raise,
for You imbue our dark with light.
I thank You that You do refresh
us mind and soul, not merely flesh.
Our souls in dreams like children go,
guileless, nightgown-clad, tiptoe,
down darkened stairs; we reach the landing.
There our angel guard is standing,
gathering us back to peace and right.
For rest, for nest, for dream's night flight,
for grace-filled dark that crowns our days,
Most Holy Sir, I give You praise!
Amen.

—JEANIE GUSHEE (1962–)

November 5

Morning

Lord of peace, Lord of joy!
Your countenance makes my heart glad.
Lord of glory, Lord of mercy, Lord of strength,
Lord of life, and of power over death,
You are Lord of lords and King of kings!
In the world there are lords many,
but to us there is but one God the Father, of whom are all things;
and one Lord Jesus Christ, by whom are all things:
to whom be all glory, who is worthy!
Amen.

—George Fox (1624–1691)

Evening

Father of Heaven,
whose goodness has brought us in safety to the close of this day . . .
another day is now gone,
and added to those for which we were before accountable.
Teach us, Almighty Father, to consider this solemn truth,
as we should do, that we may feel the importance of every day,
and every hour as it passes, and earnestly strive
to make a better use of what Thy goodness may yet bestow on us,
than we have done this time past.
We thank Thee with all our hearts for every gracious dispensation;
for all blessings that have attended our lives. . . .
Bring us in safety to the beginning of another day
and grant that we may rise again
with every serious and religious feeling which now directs us.
Amen.

—Jane Austen (1775–1817)

Morning

I beseech You, merciful God, to allow me to drink from the stream
which flows from Your fountain of life. . . .
Give me, Lord Jesus, this water,
that it may quench the burning spiritual thirst
within my soul, and purify me from all sin.
I know, King of glory, that I am asking from You a great gift.
But You give to Your faithful people without counting the cost,
and You promise even greater things in the future.
Indeed, nothing is greater than Yourself,
and You have given Yourself to mankind on the cross.
Therefore, in praying for the waters of life,
I am praying that You, the source of those waters, will give Yourself to me.
You are my light, my salvation, my food, my drink, my God.
Amen.

—COLUMBANUS (c. 550—615)

Evening

Feet, still, still now, upon the floor,
no need to hurry.
Hands, lie quietly at rest,
no task to do just now.
Body, relax in peace, serene;
now calmly rest.
Mind, let go the scurrying,
let thought be still, so still.
Soul, in silence vast as space,
reach, yearning, loving, unto God.
Amen.

—ELIZABETH SEARLE LAMB (1917—2005)

November 7

Morning

Christ, this day be within me and without me!
Christ, the lowly and meek, Christ the All-Powerful,
be in the heart of each to whom I speak,
in the mouth of each who speaks to me!
In all who draw near me, or see me, or hear me! . . .
Glory to Him who reigneth in power
the God of the elements—
Father, and Son, and Paraclete Spirit—
which Three are the One,
the ever-existing Divinity.
Amen.

—Patrick of Ireland (c. 387–c. 460)

Evening

O Lord, send down Your grace to help me,
that I may glorify Your holy name.
O Lord Jesus Christ, write the name of me, Your servant,
in the book of life, and grant me a blessed end. . . .
O Lord, grant me humility, love, and obedience.
O Lord, grant me tolerance, magnanimity, and gentleness.
O Lord, implant in me the root of all blessings:
the reverence of You in my heart. . . .
O Lord, You know Your creation,
and what You have planned for it;
may Your will also be fulfilled in me, a sinner,
for You are blessed forevermore.
Amen.

—John Chrysostom (c. 347–407)

Morning

O Prince of Life, teach us to stand more boldly on Your side,
to face the world and all our adversaries more courageously,
and not to let ourselves be dismayed by any storm of temptation;
may our eyes be steadfastly fixed on You in fearless faith;
may we trust You with perfect confidence that You will keep us, save us,
and bring us through by the power of Your grace
and the riches of Your mercy.
Amen.

—GERHARD TERSTEEGEN (1697–1769)

Evening

O Lamb of God,
who takest away the sin of the world,
look upon us and have mercy upon us;
Thou who art Thyself both victim and Priest,
Thyself both Reward and Redeemer;
keep safe from all evil
those whom Thou hast redeemed,
O Savior of the world.
Amen.

—IRENAEUS (130–202)

Morning

Arising from sleep I thank Thee, O holy Trinity;
because of the abundance of Thy goodness and long-suffering
Thou wast not wroth with me, slothful and sinful as I am;
neither hast Thou destroyed me in my transgressions:
but in Thy compassion raised me up . . .
that at dawn I might sing the glories of Thy Majesty.
Do Thou now enlighten the eyes of my understanding,
open my mouth to receive Thy words,
teach me Thy commandments, help me to do Thy will,
confessing Thee from my heart,
singing and praising Thine all-holy Name:
of the Father, and of the Son, and of the Holy Spirit:
now and ever, unto ages of ages.
Amen.

—EASTERN ORTHODOX PRAYER

Evening

Before the closing of the day
Creator, we Thee humbly pray,
That for Thy wonted mercy's sake,
Thou us under protection take.
May nothing in our minds excite
Vain dreams and phantoms of the night.
Our enemies repress, that so
Our bodies no uncleanness know.
In this, most gracious Father, hear
With Christ, Thy equal Son, our prayer;
Who with the Holy Ghost and Thee
Doth live and reign eternally.
Amen.

—CATHOLIC PRAYER (1844)

November 10

Morning

Jesus, I feel within me a great desire to please You
but, at the same time,
I feel totally incapable of doing this
without Your special light and help,
which I can expect only from You.
Accomplish Your will within me—
even in spite of me.
Amen.

—Claude La Colombière (1641–1682)

Evening

O Lord my God, my one hope, hear me,
that weariness may not lessen my will to seek You,
that I may seek Your face ever more with eager heart.
Lord, give me strength to seek You,
as You have made me to find You,
and given hope of finding You ever more and more.
My strength and my weakness are in Your hands:
preserve the one, and remedy the other.
In Your hands are my knowledge and my ignorance.
When You have opened to me,
receive my entering in.
Where You have shut,
open to my knocking.
Let me remember You,
understand You,
love You.
Increase in me all these
until You restore me
to Your perfect pattern.
Amen.

—Augustine of Hippo (354–430)

Morning

O Lord, that lends me life,
Lend me a heart replete with thankfulness.
Amen.

—WILLIAM SHAKESPEARE (1564–1616)

Evening

O good Jesus, my Master,
Teach me.
O good Jesus, Prince of peace,
Give me peace.
O good Jesus, my Refuge,
Receive me.
O good Jesus, my Pastor,
Feed my soul.
O good Jesus, Eternal Truth,
Instruct me.
O good Jesus, life of the blessed,
Make me live in Thee.
O good Jesus, Model of patience,
Comfort me.
O good Jesus, meek and humble of heart,
Make my heart like unto Thine.
O good Jesus, my Redeemer,
Save me.
O good Jesus, my God and my All,
Possess me.
O good Jesus, the true Way,
Direct me.
Amen.

—CATHOLIC PRAYER (1916)

Morning

What a good friend You are, Lord!
You are so patient, willing to wait as long as necessary
for me to turn to You.
You rejoice at the times when I love You,
but You do not hold against me the times when I ignore You.
Your patience is beyond my understanding.
Even when I pray, my mind fills with worldly concerns
and vain daydreams.
Yet You are happy if I give only a second of honest prayer,
turning that second into a seed of love.
O Lord, I enjoy Your friendship so much. . . .
Amen.

—TERESA OF ÁVILA (1515–1582)

Evening

Blessed be the Lord for another day of mercy,
even though I am now weary with its toils.
Unto the preserver of men lift I my song of gratitude . . .
my soul has learned yet more fully than ever, this day,
that there is no satisfaction to be found in earthly things—
God alone can give rest to my spirit.
As to my business, my possessions, my family, my attainments,
these are all well enough in their way,
but they cannot fulfill the desires of my immortal nature. . . .
Blessed Lord Jesus, be with me, reveal Thyself, and abide with me all night,
so that when I awake I may be still with Thee. . . .
Yes, my Lord, I present Thee my grateful acknowledgements
for tender mercies which have been new
every morning and fresh every evening; and now,
I pray Thee,
put forth Thy hand and take Thy dove into Thy bosom.
Amen.

—CHARLES SPURGEON (1834–1892)

Morning

Cause me to hear Your lovingkindness in the morning,
For in You do I trust;
Cause me to know the way in which I should walk,
For I lift up my soul to You.
Teach me to do Your will,
For You are my God;
Your Spirit is good.
Lead me in the land of uprightness.
Amen.

—Psalm 143:8, 10

Evening

Dear Jesus,
help me to spread Your fragrance everywhere I go.
Flood my soul with Your Spirit and life.
Penetrate and possess my whole being so utterly
that my life may only be a radiance of Yours.
Shine through me, and be so in me,
that every soul I come in contact with
may feel Your presence in my soul.
Let them look up and see
no longer me but only Jesus!
Stay with me, and then I shall begin to shine as You shine;
so to shine as to be a light to others.
Amen.

—Cardinal John Henry Newman (1801–1890)

Morning

O God, may Your will be done,
not only in the execution of Your commandments,
counsels, and inspirations,
which I ought to obey,
but also in suffering the afflictions
which befall me.
May Your will be done in me and by me
in everything that pleases You!
Amen.

—Francis de Sales (1567–1622)

Evening

To my weariness, O Lord, vouchsafe Thou rest,
to my exhaustion renew Thou strength.
Lighten mine eyes that I sleep not in death.
Deliver me from the terror by night,
the pestilence that walketh in darkness.
Supply me with healthy sleep,
and to pass through this night without fear.
O Keeper of Israel,
who neither slumberest nor sleepest,
guard me this night from all evil,
guard my soul, O Lord.
Amen.

—Lancelot Andrewes (1555–1626)

Morning

Dear Lord Jesus,
I give You my hands to do Your work;
I give You my feet to go Your way;
I give You my eyes to see as You see;
I give You my tongue to speak Your words;
I give You my mind that You may think in me;
I give You my spirit that You may pray in me.
Above all I give You my heart that You may love in me—
love God the Father and love all humankind.
I give You my whole self, Lord Jesus,
that You may grow in me,
so that it is You who lives, works, and prays in me.
Amen.

—THE GRAIL PRAYER, ANONYMOUS

Evening

Lord, teach me to number my days,
that I may apply my heart unto wisdom.
Lighten, if it be Thy will,
the pressures of this world's cares.
Above all, reconcile me to Thy will,
and give me a peace which the world cannot take away;
through Jesus Christ our Lord.
Amen.

—THOMAS CHALMERS (1780–1847)

November 16

Morning

Source of all good! Day by day Thy blessings are renewed to me.
With reverent and thankful heart I come
to seek the blessed sense of Thy presence. . . .
O that I, too, could be reborn with the morning. . . .
I remember my thoughtless life, my impatient temper, my selfish aims.
Yet I know that Thou hast neither made me blind,
like the creatures that have no sin,
nor left me without holy guidance.
Thy still small voice speaks in my inmost conscience,
and appeals to me to choose the better part.
O true and only God, take me now to serve Thee in newness of spirit. . . .
sweep away with a holy breath every trace of fear, care,
or an uncharitable mind. . . .
May I ever grow in purity and goodness, in love to Thee,
and devotion to Thy holy will.
Amen.

—JAMES MARTINEAU (1805–1900)

Evening

Write Thy blessed name, O Lord, upon my heart,
there to remain so indelibly engraved,
that no prosperity, no adversity
shall ever move me from Thy love.
Be Thou to me a strong tower of defence,
a comforter in tribulation,
a deliverer in distress,
a very present help in trouble,
and a guide to heaven
through the many temptations and dangers of this life.
Amen.

—THOMAS À KEMPIS (1380–1471)

Morning

Give ear to my words, O Lord,
Consider my meditation.
Give heed to the voice of my cry,
My King and my God,
For to You I will pray.
My voice You shall hear in the morning, O Lord;
In the morning I will direct it to You,
And will look up.
For You are not a God who takes pleasure in wickedness,
Nor shall evil dwell with You.
But let all those rejoice who put their trust in You;
Let them ever shout for joy, because You defend them;
Let those also who love Your name
Be joyful in You.
For You, O Lord, will bless the righteous;
With favor You will surround him as with a shield.
Amen.

—Psalm 5:1–4, 11–12

Evening

Let me not seek out of Thee what I can find only in Thee, O Lord:
peace and rest and joy and bliss, which abide in Thee alone.
Lift up my soul above the weary round
of harassing thoughts to Thy eternal presence.
Lift up my mind to the pure, bright, serene light of Thy presence,
that there I may repose in Thy love and be at rest from myself
and all things that weary me;
and thence return, arrayed in Thy peace,
to do and bear whatsoever
shall best please Thee, O blessed Lord.
Amen.

—Edward Bouverie Pusey (1800–1882)

NOVEMBER 18

Morning

Since it is of Thy mercy, O gracious Father,
that another day is added to my life;
I here dedicate both my soul and body to Thee and Thy service,
in a sober, righteous, and godly life:
in which resolution, do Thou, O merciful God,
confirm and strengthen me;
that, as I grow in age, I may grow in grace,
and in the knowledge of my Lord and Savior Jesus Christ.
Amen.

—*Book of Common Prayer* (1928)

Evening

My Lord and my God
I have realized that whoever undertakes to do anything
for the sake of earthly things
or to earn the praise of others deceives himself.
Today one thing pleases the world,
tomorrow another.
What is praised on one occasion
is denounced on another.
Blessed be You,
my Lord and my God,
for You are unchangeable for all eternity.
Whoever serves You faithfully to the end
will enjoy life without end in eternity.
Amen.

—Thérèse of Lisieux (1873–1897)

Morning

Lord, help me to live this day quietly, easily.
Help me to lean upon Thy great strength trustfully, restfully,
to wait for the unfolding of Thy will patiently, serenely,
to meet others peacefully, joyously,
to face tomorrow, confidently, courageously.
Amen.

—ANONYMOUS

Evening

Loving, omnipotent God,
the praise that I can render
is only a poor portion of all the
honor and blessing which to You are due.
My limitations You well know.
But just as one bird does not make
all the music of the night, so too with praise.
Here in this evening hour it pleases me
to think of my prayer ascending along with
the prayers, some relaxed murmurs, some fervent cries,
of thousands of praying souls throughout the world.
(How great You are that You can hear us all!)
I join this worldwide chorus of Your faithful
and proclaim: holy are You! Most blessed are You!
Amen.

—JEANIE GUSHEE (1962–)

Morning

Lord, grant me a holy heart that sees always what is fine and pure,
and is not frightened at the sight of sin, but creates order wherever it goes.
Grant me a heart that knows nothing of boredom, weeping and sighing.
Let me not be overly concerned with the bothersome thing I call "myself."
Lord, give me a sense of humor,
and I will feel happiness in life and give profit to others.
Amen.

—Sir Thomas More (1478–1535)

Evening

O Lord God. . . .
I desire to thank You, that I am this day a living witness
to testify that You are a God that will ever vindicate
the cause of the poor and needy,
and that You have always proved Yourself to be a friend and Father to me.
O, continue Your loving kindness even unto the end;
and when health and strength begin to decay,
and I, as it were, draw nigh unto Thy grace,
O then afford me your heart-cheering presence,
and enable me to rely entirely upon You.
Never leave me nor forsake me,
but have mercy upon me for Your great name's sake.
And not for myself alone do I ask these blessings,
but for all the poor and needy, all widows and fatherless children,
and for the stranger in distress; and may they call upon You
in such a manner as to be convinced
that You are a prayer-hearing and prayer-answering God;
and Thine shall be the praise, forever.
Amen.

—Maria W. Stewart (1803–1879)

Morning

Loving Father,
I invite You into my life today,
and make myself available to You.
Help me to become the best-version-of-myself,
by seeking Your will
and by being a living example of Your love in the world.
Open my heart to areas of my life that need to change,
so I can carry out the mission You have imagined for my life and
experience the joy You desire for me.
Inspire me to live the Christian faith in ways that are
dynamic and engaging.
Show me how to best get involved in the life of my parish.
Give our community a hunger for best practices
and continuous learning.
Give me courage when I am afraid,
hope when I am discouraged,
and clarity in times of decision.
Lead Your Church to become all You imagined it would be
for the people of our times.
Amen.

—MATTHEW KELLY (1973–)

Evening

O my God! Blessed Trinity,
I desire to love You and to make You loved.
Amen.

—THÉRÈSE OF LISIEUX (1873–1897)

Morning

Use me, then, my Savior, for whatever purpose,
and in whatever way, Thou mayest require.
Here is my poor heart, an empty vessel;
fill it with Thy grace.
Here is my sinful and troubled soul;
quicken it and refresh it with Thy love.
Take my heart for Thine abode;
my mouth to spread abroad the glory of Thy name;
my love and all my powers,
for the advancement of Thy believing people;
and never suffer the steadfastness and confidence of my faith to abate;
so that at all times I may be enabled from the heart to say,
"Jesus needs me, and I am His."
Amen.

—Dwight L. Moody (1837–1899)

Evening

Lord, bless me
with all heavenly benediction,
and make me pure and holy in Your sight.
May the riches of Your glory abound in me. . . .
instruct me with the Word of truth,
inform me with the gospel of salvation,
and enrich me with Your love,
through Jesus Christ, our Lord.
Amen.

—Gelasian Sacramentary (8th c.)

NOVEMBER 23

Morning

Lord Jesus Christ,
pierce my soul with Thy love so that I may always long for Thee alone,
who art . . . the fulfillment of the soul's deepest desires. . . .
May I always seek and find Thee,
think upon Thee, speak to Thee,
and do all things for the honour and glory of Thy holy Name.
Be always . . . my peace, my refuge and my help
in whom my heart is rooted
so that I may never be separated from Thee.
Amen.

—BONAVENTURE (1217–1274)

Evening

How great is Your goodness, dear Lord!
Blessed are You for ever!
May all created things praise You, O God,
for loving us so much that we can truthfully speak
of Your fellowship with mankind,
even in this earthly exile.
And however virtuous we may be,
our virtue always depends on Your great warmth
and generosity, dear Lord.
Your bounty is infinite.
How wonderful are Your works!
Amen.

—TERESA OF ÁVILA (1515–1582)

NOVEMBER 24: FEAST OF CHRIST THE KING

Morning

O Jesus, Christ, I acknowledge You as universal King.
Exercise all Your rights over me.
I renew my baptismal vows,
I renounce Satan, his pomp and his works;
I promise to live as a good Christian.
And, in particular do I pledge myself to labor . . .
that all hearts may acknowledge
Your sacred kingship, and that thus the reign
of Your peace may be established
throughout the whole universe.
Amen.

—TRADITIONAL CATHOLIC PRAYER

Evening

Almighty and everlasting God,
whose will it is to restore all things
in Thy well-beloved Son,
the King of kings and Lord of lords:
mercifully grant that the peoples of the earth,
divided and enslaved by sin,
may be freed and brought together
under His most gracious rule;
who liveth and reigneth with Thee and the Holy Spirit,
one God, now and for ever.
Amen.

—BOOK OF COMMON PRAYER (1979)

Morning

Keep me, Lord, attentive at prayer,
temperate in food and drink,
diligent in my work,
firm in my intentions.
Let my conscience be clear,
my conduct without fault,
my speech blameless,
my life well-ordered.
Put me on guard against my human weaknesses.
Let me cherish Your love for me,
keep Your law, and come at last to Your salvation.
Teach me to be aware that this world is passing,
that my true future is the happiness of heaven,
that life on earth is short,
and the life to come eternal.
Amen.

—Pope Clement XI (1649–1721)

Evening

God the Father, bless us;
God the Son, defend us;
God the Spirit, keep us
now and evermore.
Amen.

—E. Jahsmann, *Little Folded Hands* (1959)

Morning

Almighty God, more generous than any father,
we stand amazed at the many gifts You shower upon us.
You give freely and willingly, always with regard to our ability to receive.
You give daily gifts, teaching us to trust You for tomorrow.
You give us gifts through one another, so that we may learn to share.
You give through our own effort, respecting our independence.
How thoughtfully You offer all Your gifts!
So continue, Lord, in Your goodness.
Amen.

—Anonymous

Evening

O Christ my Lord,
my day ends with so much left undone.
But so too will my life—
when I sleep earth's final sleep.
I cherish the illusion
that I am writing my own story,
which will conclude at my direction,
when I have fulfilled all my intention.
But no—You are composing, in my few days,
the story You desire.
Ceding my illusion,
I release myself into Your care.
In trust, I close my eyes in sleep.

—David P. Gushee (1962–)

Morning

We were enclosed,
O eternal Father,
within the garden of Your bosom.
You drew us out of Your holy mind
like a flower
petalled with our soul's three powers . . .
You gave us memory
so that we might be able to hold Your blessings
and show forth the flower of glory to Your name
and the fruit of profit to ourselves.
You gave us understanding to understand Your truth
and Your will—
Your will that wants only that we be made holy—
so that we might bear first the flower of glory
and then the fruit of virtue.
And You gave us Your will
so that we might be able to love
what our understanding has seen
and what our memory has held.
For this, we praise and thank You.
Amen.

—Catherine of Siena (1347–1380)

Evening

O Lord, my God, grant me Your peace;
already, indeed, You have made me rich in all things!
Give me that peace of being at rest,
that Sabbath peace,
the peace which knows no end.
Amen.

—Augustine of Hippo (354–430)

November 28: Thanksgiving Day

Morning

Come, ye thankful people, come
Raise the song of harvest home!
All is safely gathered in,
'Ere the winter storms begin;
God, the Maker, doth provide
For our wants to be supplied;
Come to God's own temple, come;
Raise the song of harvest home.
Amen.

—Henry Alford (1810–1871)

Evening

Let us give thanks to God our Father
for all His gifts so freely bestowed upon us.
For the beauty and wonder of Your creation,
in earth and sky and sea, we thank You, Lord.
For all that is gracious in the lives of men and women,
revealing the image of Christ, we thank You, Lord.
For our daily food and drink, our homes and families, and our friends,
we thank You, Lord.
For minds to think, and hearts to love, and hands to serve,
we thank You, Lord. . . .
Above all, we give You thanks for the great mercies
and promises given to us in Christ Jesus our Lord;
to Him be praise and glory,
with You, O Father, and the Holy Spirit, now and for ever.
Amen.

—Book of Common Prayer (1979)

Morning

Praise to God, immortal praise
For the love that crowns our days! . . .
For the blessings of the field,
For the stores the gardens yield . . .
All that liberal Autumn pours
From her rich o'erflowing stores;
Thanks, to Thee, our God, we owe,
Source whence all our blessings flow!
And for these our souls shall raise
Grateful vows and solemn praise.
Amen.

—Anna Letitia Barbauld (1743–1825)

Evening

Thou hast, with ever watchful eye,
Looked down on us with holy care,
And from Thy storehouse in the sky
Hast scattered plenty everywhere.
Then we lift up our songs of praise
To Thee, O Father, good and kind;
To Thee we consecrate our days;
Be Thine the temple of each mind.
With incense sweet our thanks ascend;
Before Thy works our powers pall;
Though we should strive years without end,
We could not thank Thee for them all.
Amen.

—Paul Laurence Dunbar (1872–1906)

Morning

Accept, O Lord, our thanks and praise for all that You have done for us.
We thank You for the splendor of the whole creation,
for the beauty of this world,
for the wonder of life, and for the mystery of love.
We thank You for the blessing of family and friends,
and for the loving care which surrounds us on every side.
We thank You for setting us at tasks which demand our best efforts,
and for leading us to accomplishments which satisfy and delight us. . . .
Above all we thank You for Your Son Jesus Christ;
for the truth of His Word and the example of His life;
for His steadfast obedience, by which He overcame temptation;
for His dying, through which He overcame death;
and for His rising to life again, in which we are raised
to the life of Your kingdom.
Grant us the gift of Your Spirit, that we may know Him
and make Him known;
and through Him, at all times and in all places,
may give thanks to You in all things.
Amen.

—*Book of Common Prayer* (1979)

Evening

O most loving heart of Jesus,
I commend to You this night my heart and soul
that they may rest peacefully in You.
Since I cannot praise You while I sleep,
may my guardian angel replace me,
that all my heart's beats may be so many acts of praise and thanksgiving
offered to Your loving heart and that of Your eternal Father.
Amen.

—Maria Soledad Torres Acosta (1826–1887)

ADVENT

Advent begins four Sundays before Christmas and ends on Christmas Eve. During Advent we "wait in joyful hope for the coming of our Savior Jesus Christ," in the phrase used each week in the Catholic Mass. Advent is about Jesus' coming; even the word *advent* means "coming." We celebrate the threefold coming of Jesus. We remember His coming in the past as a baby in Bethlehem, born to redeem the world. We are thankful for His coming into our hearts in the present, as we make more and more of our lives available to Him, to be used as He wishes. And we look forward joyfully to His Second Coming at the end of time when all people shall be judged and all creation shall be purified and perfected.

The Christmas story is, simply put, the most beautiful story in the world. The four lovely weeks of Advent allow us to take this story out each year and examine it. Like a jewel that sparkles in different colors when it is held up to the light and rotated, Advent lets us see the Christmas story from different angles. We sense the longing of the prophets who foretold Christ; our hearts wonder with Mary, rejoice with Elizabeth, empathize with Joseph, and thrill with the shepherds.

Advent reminds us, too, that while Christmas was glorious, it was human sinfulness and estrangement from God that made it necessary for Jesus to come to earth. So we are reminded of our spiritual lives, and of our need to be found walking in righteousness when He comes again in glory. Mostly Advent gives us a chance to remember and pay homage to the most beautiful part of the Christmas story: the incomparable, miracle-working, ardent, relational, self-sacrificing love of God for the people of the world.

THE ANNUNCIATION

December 1: First Sunday of Advent

Morning

Most gracious Lord, by whose direction this time
is appointed for renewing
the memory of Thy infinite mercy to man
in the incarnation of Thy only Son,
grant that I may live this holy time in the spirit of thanksgiving,
and every day raise up my heart to Thee in the grateful acknowledgement
of what Thou hast done for us.
Besides this, I ask Thy grace, O God,
that I may make a due use of this holy time,
for preparing my soul to receive Christ our Lord
coming into the world at the approaching solemnity of Christmas.
Christ came into the world to do good to all. . . .
in all things, O God, may I follow the spirit of charity,
being forward in bringing comfort and relief to all,
as far as their circumstances shall require, and mine permit.
Grant, O Lord, that I may prepare to meet our Redeemer.
Amen.

—John Goter (1650–1704)

Evening

Merciful God,
who sent Thy messengers the prophets to preach repentance
and prepare the way for our salvation:
give us grace to heed their warnings and forsake our sins,
that we may greet with joy the coming of Jesus Christ our Redeemer;
who liveth and reigneth with Thee and the Holy Spirit,
one God, now and for ever.
Amen.

—Book of Common Prayer (1979)

Morning

O Lord Jesus Christ, King of glory, King of kings and Lord of lords,
the Son of the living God and Son of David, come.
Come now to Your Church that You have purchased with Your blood.
Come with Your gracious presence that we may rejoice in You.
Come with Your love, humility, and perfect obedience,
and let Your lowliness become our glory.
Come into the midst of Your people and bless us, for we are Your heritage.
Forgive us our sin, and do not angrily cast away Your servants,
for You are meek and gracious.
Clothe us with the garment of Your righteousness,
for You are the only righteous one and our helper.
Satisfy us with the abundance of Your mercy,
for You did become poor for our sakes,
that by Your poverty we might be made rich.
Hear us, Lord Jesus, for the sake of Your holy name.
Amen.

—MARTIN LUTHER (1483–1546)

Evening

May the Lamb of God, who once came to take away the sins of the world,
take away from us every stain of sin. Amen.
And may He who came to redeem what was lost, at His second coming
not cast away what He has redeemed. Amen.
That, when He comes, we may have perpetual joy with
Him on whom we have believed. Amen.

—MOZARABIC BREVIARY (1502)

Morning

O King of the nations, You are the headstone
of the glorious hall of creation.
You are the firm mortar which holds the building together.
Throughout the earth people marvel at Your works. . . .
O just and faithful King, You can unlock the prison-house of sin,
and let us out into the glorious freedom of love.
Now we sit in darkness, grieving over the wrongs we have committed.
We long for the sun, we yearn for the warmth
and brightness of Your truth. . . .
Come now, high King of heaven. Come to us in flesh and bone. . . .
Bring peace to us. . . .
Do not forget us, but show mercy on us.
Impart to us Your everlasting joy,
so that we, who are fashioned by Your hands,
may praise Your glory.
Amen.

—THE EXETER BOOK (c. 950)

Evening

All powerful God,
increase our strength of will for doing good,
that Christ may find an eager welcome at His coming,
and call us to His side in the Kingdom of Heaven,
where He lives and reigns with You and the Holy Spirit,
one God, forever and ever.
Amen.

—ROMAN SACRAMENTARY (20TH c.)

December 4: Advent

Morning

You are our eternal salvation, the unfailing life of the world.
Light everlasting, You are truly our redemption.
Grieving that the human race was perishing through the tempter's power,
without leaving the heights You came to the depths in Your loving kindness.
Readily taking our humanity by Your own gracious will,
You saved all earthly creatures, long since lost, restoring joy to the world.
Redeem our souls and our bodies, O Christ,
and so possess us as Your shining dwellings.
By Your first coming, make us righteous;
at Your second coming, set us free:
so that, when the world is filled with light and You judge all things,
we may be clad in spotless robes and follow in Your steps, O King,
into the heavenly hall.
Amen.

—Anonymous (10th c.)

Evening

Come, true light. Come, life eternal.
Come, hidden mystery. . . . Come, reality beyond all words.
Come, person beyond all understanding. Come, rejoicing without end.
Come, light that knows no evening.
Come, unfailing expectation of the saved.
Come, raising of the fallen. Come, resurrection of the dead.
Come, all-powerful, for unceasingly You create. . . .
Come, for Your name fills our hearts with longing
and is ever on our lips. . . .
Come, for You are Yourself the desire that is within me.
Come, the consolation of my humble soul.
Come, my joy, my endless delight.
Amen.

—Symeon the New Theologian (949–1022)

Morning

God of power and mercy,
open my heart in welcome.
Remove the things that hinder me from receiving Christ with joy,
so that I may share His wisdom,
and become one with Him when He comes in glory,
for He lives and reigns with You and the Holy Spirit,
one God, for ever and ever.
Amen.

—Roman Sacramentary (20th c.)

Evening

I beseech Thee, Almighty God,
to purify my conscience by Thy daily visitation,
that when Your Son Jesus Christ my Lord
comes He may find in me a mansion swept clean,
prepared for Himself;
who lives and reigns with Thee and the Holy Spirit,
One God, now and forever.
Amen.

—Gelasian Sacramentary (8th c.)

December 6: Advent

Morning

Father in Heaven,
my heart desires the warmth of Your love
and my mind is searching for the light of Your Word.
Increase my longing for Christ our Saviour,
and give me the strength to grow in love,
that the dawn of His coming
may find me rejoicing in His presence
and welcoming the light of His truth.
Amen.

—ROMAN MISSAL

Evening

Good Jesu, born at this time,
a little child for love of us;
be Thou born in me, that I may
be a little child in love of Thee,
and hang on Thy love as on my
mother's bosom,
trustfully, lovingly, peacefully;
hushing all my cares in love of Thee.
Good Jesu, sweeten every thought of mine
with the sweetness of Thy love.
Good Jesu, give me a deep love for Thee,
that nothing may be too hard for me
to bear for love of Thee.
Amen.

—EDWARD BOUVERIE PUSEY (1800–1882)

December 7: Advent

Morning

Thou hast made me, O Lord, when I was not,
and that according to Thine own image.
Thou from the very first instant of my being has been
my God,
my Father,
my Deliverer, and
all my good.
Thou, with the benefits of Thy providence, hast preserved my life
even till this present.
O, let it be spent in Thy service!
But because these things, O gracious Lord, cost Thee nothing,
to bind me more fast to Thee, Thou wouldst need give me a present
bought by Thee most dearly.
Thou hast come down from heaven, to seek me in all those ways
in which I had lost myself.
O, draw up my soul unto Thee!
Amen.

—Augustine Baker (1575–1641)

Evening

God, who makest us glad with the yearly remembrance
of the birth of Thy only Son Jesus Christ,
grant that as we joyfully receive Him for our Redeemer,
so we may with sure confidence behold Him, when He shall come to be
our Judge, who liveth and reigneth with You and the Holy Spirit,
world without end.
Amen.

—Book of Common Prayer (1549)

THE VISITATION

Morning

God of love and mercy,
help me to follow the example of Mary,
who was always ready to do Your will.
At the message of an angel she welcomed Your eternal Son.
I pray that following the example of her who was filled
with the light of the Spirit
and became the temple of Your Word,
I may humbly hold fast to Your will.
Amen.

—ROMAN SACRAMENTARY (20TH C.)

Evening

Christ our God Incarnate,
whose Virgin Mother was blessed in bearing Thee,
but still more blessed in keeping Thy word;
grant us, who honour the exaltation of her lowliness,
to follow the example of her devotion to Thy will,
who livest, and reignest with the Father and the Holy Spirit,
one God, now and for ever.
Amen.

—WILLIAM BRIGHT (1824–1901)

Morning

Jesus,
You are our King and Savior,
and You draw near!
O come let us adore You!
Give us grace to cast away the works of darkness,
and put on Your armor of Light.
Then when You come in glory may we rise to meet You in eternal life.
Help us, Lord, learn Your ways and walk in Your paths.
We wait with hope for the day when
"the glory of the Lord shall be revealed,
and all flesh shall see it together."
Amen.

—ANONYMOUS

Evening

Almighty God, who hast given us Thy only begotten Son
to take our nature upon Him,
and as at this time to be born of a pure Virgin;
grant that I being regenerate,
and made Thy child by adoption and grace,
may daily be renewed by Thy holy Spirit;
through the same our Lord Jesus Christ,
who liveth and reigneth with Thee, and the same Spirit,
ever one God, world without end.
Amen.

—BOOK OF COMMON PRAYER (1549)

Morning

What is this jewel that is so precious?
I can see it has been quarried not by men, but by God.
It is You, dear Jesus.
You have been dug from the rocks of Heaven itself
to be offered to me as a gift beyond price.
You shine in the darkness.
Every colour of the rainbow can be seen within You.
The whole earth is bathed in Your light.
Infant Jesus, by being born as man
You have taken upon Yourself the pain of death.
But such a jewel can never be destroyed.
You are immortal.
And by defying Your own death, You shall deliver me from death.
Amen.

—Adam of St. Victor (12th c.)

Evening

Be near me, Lord Jesus;
I ask Thee to stay
Close by me forever,
And love me, I pray.
Bless all the dear children
In Thy tender care.
And fit us for Heaven
To live with Thee there.
Amen.

—Martin Luther (1483–1546)

DECEMBER 11: ADVENT

Morning

Come, Thou long expected Jesus,
Born to set Thy people free;
From our fears and sins release us,
Let us find our rest in Thee.
Israel's strength and consolation,
Hope of all the earth Thou art;
Dear desire of every nation,
Joy of every longing heart.
Born Thy people to deliver,
Born a child and yet a King,
Born to reign in us forever,
Now Thy gracious kingdom bring.
By Thine own eternal Spirit
Rule in all our hearts alone;
By Thine all sufficient merit,
Raise us to Thy glorious throne.
Amen.

—CHARLES WESLEY (1707–1788)

Evening

O Thou, who hast foretold that Thou wilt return to judgment
in an hour that we are not aware of:
grant us grace to watch and pray always;
that whether Thou shalt come at evening, or at midnight, or in the morning,
we may be found among the number of those servants
who shall be blessed in watching for their Lord;
to whom be all glory, now and for evermore.
Amen.

—*NON-JURORS PRAYER BOOK* (1734)

December 12: Advent

Morning

O God, our Father,
I thank You that You sent Your Son Jesus Christ into this world to be
our Savior and our Lord.
I thank You that He took our body and our flesh and blood upon Himself,
and so showed us that this body of ours is fit to be Your dwelling-place. . . .
Lord Jesus, come again to us this day.
Come into our hearts, and so cleanse them,
that we being pure in heart may see God, our Father.
Come into our minds, and so enlighten and illumine them
that we may know You who are the way, the truth, and the life.
Amen.

—William Barclay (1907–1978)

Evening

We remember Thy love, O Jesus, as it was manifest to us in Thy holy life,
from the manger of Bethlehem to the garden of Gethsemane.
We track Thee from the cradle to the grave—
for every word and deed of Thine was love—
and we rejoice in Thy love, which death did not exhaust;
Thy love which shone resplendent in Thy resurrection.
We remember that burning fire of love
which will never let Thee hold Thy peace
until Thy chosen ones be all safely housed.
Amen.

—Charles Spurgeon (1834–1892)

Morning

Lord Jesus,
Master of both the light and the darkness,
send Your Holy Spirit upon our preparations for Christmas.
We, who have so much to do,
seek quiet spaces to hear Your voice each day.
We, who are anxious over many things,
look forward to Your coming among us.
We, who are blessed in so many ways,
long for the complete joy of Your kingdom. . . .
We are Your people, walking in darkness,
yet seeking the light.
To You we say, "Come, Lord Jesus!"
Amen.

—MARK NEILSEN (2002)

Evening

Almighty God,
give me grace that I may cast away the works of darkness,
and put upon me the armour of light
now in the time of this mortal life
in which Thy Son Jesus Christ came to visit us in great humility;
that in the last day, when He shall come again in His glorious Majesty,
to judge both the quick and the dead,
I may rise to the life immortal,
through Him who liveth and reigneth with Thee and the Holy Ghost,
now and ever.
Amen.

—BOOK OF COMMON PRAYER (1549)

Morning

Come, long-expected Jesus.
Excite in me the joy and love and peace
it is right to bring to the manger of my Lord.
Raise in me, too, sober reverence
for the God who acted there,
hearty gratitude for the life begun there,
and spirited resolution to serve the Father and Son.
I pray in the name of Jesus Christ,
whose advent I hail.
Amen.

—CATHOLIC PRAYER

Evening

Lord Jesus, You are the light of the world.
Come, Lord Jesus.
You are light in our darkness.
Come, Lord Jesus.
Son of God, save us from our sins.
Come, Lord Jesus.
Bring hope into the lives of all people.
Come, Lord Jesus.
Give Your peace to all nations.
Come, Lord Jesus.
Be the joy of all who love You.
Come, Lord Jesus.
Amen.

—ADVENT LITANY

December 15: Third Sunday of Advent

Morning

Merciful and most loving God,
by whose will and bountiful gift Jesus Christ our Lord humbled Himself
that He might exalt humankind;
and became flesh that He might restore in us the most celestial image;
and was born of the Virgin that he might uplift the lowly:
grant us the inheritance of the meek,
perfect in us Your likeness,
and bring us at last to rejoice in beholding Your beauty,
and, with all Your saints to glory in Your grace;
through the same Jesus Christ our Lord.
Amen.

—Gallican Sacramentary (7th c.)

Evening

It is the season of darkness.
Day hardly dawns before night again falls.
And so too the world—
we catch glimpses of day, of sun, of warmth
against the backdrop of darkness, cold, and gray.
Whether or not they acknowledge it,
everyone looks for the Light of the world
(or light in the world).
Some wait in confident expectation—
others wait in quiet desperation.
This night
I close my eyes in the darkness
and yearn for Your Light,
brighter than a thousand suns.
Amen.

—David P. Gushee (1962–)

Morning

Let me have a clean heart ready inside me for the Lord Jesus,
so that He will be glad to come in,
gratefully accepting the hospitality of that world, my heart:
He whose glory and power will endure throughout the ages.
Amen.

—ORIGEN (185–254)

Evening

O Divine Infant of Bethlehem, whom I adore
and acknowledge to be my sovereign Lord,
come and take birth in my heart. Amen.
O Sovereign Jesus, grant that each moment of my life, I may
pay homage to that moment in which Thou didst begin
the work of our salvation. Amen. . . .
Savior and Redeemer, with all earnestness and respect, I pay
homage to that charity, humility, and bounty that Thou didst
display in Thy Infancy, graciously undertaken for love of us. . . .
Give me grace to . . . serve Thee with fidelity, as a servant,
all the days of my life, and to obtain a happy death . . .
to praise and bless Thy divine mercies forever and ever. Amen.
Lord, I meditate on these words:
"Whilst deep silence dwelt on all things below,
and the night was in the midst of its course,
the almighty Word came down from His throne. Alleluia."
Amen.

—TRADITIONAL CATHOLIC NOVENA (ADAPTED)

DECEMBER 17: ADVENT

O Lord, our King and our Savior!
Let us celebrate this festival without false ideas, but with our hearts open
to receive Your Word, Your promise, Your commandment.
Our grumbles and doubts,
our errors and mistakes,
our stubbornness and defiance
should trouble us even during these days of joy, because they trouble You.
But as we rejoice at Your birth in the world, we ask You to accept us
and uplift us as we are.
And we pray that, in Your strength,
we shall be willing to be counted amongst the poor and humble,
as You counted Yourself.
Amen.

—KARL BARTH (1886–1968)

Evening

O Wisdom, coming forth from the mouth of the Most High,
and reaching mightily from one end of the earth
to the other, ordering all things well:
come and teach us the way of prudence. . . .
O Daystar, splendor of light eternal
and sun of righteousness:
come and enlighten those who dwell in darkness
and the shadow of death. . . .
O Emmanuel, our King and Lawgiver,
the desire of all nations and their Savior:
come and save us, O Lord our God.
Amen.

—CATHOLIC LITURGY (9TH C.)

Morning

O Lord Jesus Christ,
who didst humble Thyself to become man,
and to be born into the world for our salvation;
teach me the grace of humility,
root out of my heart all pride and haughtiness,
and so fashion me after Thy holy likeness in this world,
that in the world to come I may be made like unto Thee;
for Thine own name's and mercy's sake.
Amen.

—WILLIAM WALSHAM HOW (1823–1897)

Evening

To Thee, O Christ, O Word of the Father,
I offer up my lowly praises and unfeigned hearty thanks:
who for love of our fallen race didst most wonderfully
and humbly choose to be made man,
and to take our nature as never more to lay it by;
so that we might be born again by the Spirit
and restored in the image of God;
to whom, one blessed Trinity, be ascribed all honor, might,
majesty, and dominion,
now and for ever.
Amen.

—LANCELOT ANDREWES (1555–1626)

December 19: Advent

Morning

God of love and truth,
You loved the world so much that You sent Your only Son to be our Savior.
From a Virgin You brought Him forth for the world to see.
May I receive Him as my Lord and Brother,
and celebrate Him as my gracious Redeemer.
I give You thanks for my salvation and for all Your gifts.
Amen.

—Roman Sacramentary (20th c.)

Evening

We do not proclaim only one coming of Christ,
but a second as well, and that much more glorious than the first.
For the first bore with it the sign of suffering;
the second will confer the diadem of the divine kingdom.
For He was born from God before all ages;
and He was born from a Virgin in the consummation of time.
He came hidden like rain upon a fleece;
He will come in the lateness of days, manifest to all creation.
At His first coming He was wrapped in swaddling cloths in a manger.
At His second coming He shall be garbed in the vestments of heavenly light.
In His first coming He endured the cross and was spurned in shame;
in His second coming He will be glorified, in the company of hosts of angels.
Therefore we repose not only in the first coming, Lord,
but we eagerly await the second.
At the first coming we said, "Blessed is He who comes
in the name of the Lord."
At the second we shall say it again, when with the angels
we shall rush to greet Thee.
And we will cry out in adoration,
"Blessed is He who comes in the name of the Lord!"
Amen.

—Cyril of Jerusalem (315–386)

Morning

Let kindness go from us to others with every gift,
and good desires with every Christmas greeting.
Deliver us from evil by the blessing which Christ brings,
and teach us to be merry with a clear heart.
May the Christmas morning make us happy to be Thy children,
and the Christmas evening bring us to our beds with grateful thoughts,
forgiving and forgiven, for Jesus' sake.
Amen.

—ROBERT LOUIS STEVENSON (1850–1894)

Evening

Lord Jesus Christ, Savior of the world,
You became man to give us a life in abundance.
You promised to remain with Your Church until the end of time.
Then Your kingdom will come,
a new heaven and a new earth,
full of love, justice, and peace.
This is our hope, our foundation.
Thanks be to You, O Lord.
Amen.

—CATHOLIC PRAYER

December 21: Advent

Morning

Come, O Thou eternal light, salvation, comfort,
be our light in darkness,
our salvation in life,
our comfort in death;
and lead us in the straight way to everlasting life,
that we may praise Thee, for ever.
Amen.

—Bernhard Albrecht (1569–1636)

Evening

Lord Jesus Christ, be present now;
Our hearts in true devotion bow,
Your Spirit send with light divine,
And let Your truth within us shine.
Unseal our lips to sing Your praise
In endless hymns through all our days.
Increase our faith and light our minds;
And set us free from doubt that blinds.
Then shall we join the hosts that cry
"O holy, holy Lord Most High!"
And in the light of that blessed place
We then shall see You face to face.
All glory to the Father, Son,
And Holy Spirit, Three in One!
To You, O blessed Trinity,
Be praise throughout eternity!
Amen.

—Wilhelm IV of Sachsen-Weimar (1598–1662); translated by
Catherine Winkworth (1827–1878)

Morning

The feast day of Your birth resembles You, Lord,
because it brings joy to all humanity.
Old people and infants alike enjoy Your day.
Your day is celebrated from generation to generation.
Kings and emperors may pass away,
and the festivals to commemorate them soon lapse.
But Your festival will be remembered till the end of time.
Your day is a means and a pledge of peace.
At Your birth heaven and earth were reconciled;
since You came from Heaven to earth on that day
You forgave our sins and wiped away our guilt.
You gave us so many gifts on Your birthday:
A treasure chest of spiritual medicines for the sick;
spiritual light for those that are blind;
the cup of salvation for the thirsty;
the bread of life for the hungry.
In the winter when trees are bare,
You give us the most succulent spiritual fruit.
In the frost when the earth is barren,
You bring new hope to our souls.
In December when seeds are hidden in the soil,
the staff of life springs forth from the virgin womb.
Amen.

— EPHRAIM THE SYRIAN (c. 305–373)

Evening

Ah, dearest Jesus, holy Child,
Make Thee a bed, soft, undefiled,
Within my heart, that it may be
A quiet chamber kept for Thee.
Amen.

— MARTIN LUTHER (1483–1546)

DECEMBER 23: ADVENT

Morning

Let Your goodness, Lord,
appear to us, that we, made in Your image,
conform ourselves to it.
In our own strength we cannot imitate Your majesty, power and wonder;
nor is it fitting for us to try.
But Your mercy reaches from the Heavens,
through the clouds, to the earth below.
You have come to us as a small child,
but You have brought us the greatest of all gifts,
the gift of eternal love.
Caress us with Your tiny hands, embrace us with Your tiny arms,
and pierce our hearts with Your soft, sweet cries.
Amen.

—BERNARD OF CLAIRVAUX (1090–1153)

Evening

Lift up your heads, you mighty gates;
Behold, the King of Glory waits;
The King of kings is drawing near;
The Savior of the world is here!
Fling wide the portals of your heart;
Make it a temple, set apart
From earthly use for heaven's employ,
Adorned with prayer and love and joy.
Redeemer come, with us abide;
Our hearts to You we open wide;
Let us Your inner presence feel;
Your grace and love in us reveal.
Your Holy Spirit lead us on
Until our glorious goal is won;
Eternal praise, eternal fame
Be offered, Savior, to Your name!
Amen.

—GEORGE WEISSEL (1590–1635)

December 24: Christmas Eve

Morning

Almighty God, Father of Light,
a Child is born for us, and a Son is given to us.
Your eternal Word leaped down from Heaven
in the silent watches of the night,
and now we, Your Church, are filled with wonder
at the nearness of our God!
Open our hearts to receive the Savior's life,
and increase our vision with the rising of the dawn
that our lives may be filled with His glory and peace,
who lives and reigns forever,
Amen.

—Catholic Liturgy

Evening

Lord Jesus, for eternities now,
heaven and earth, like fond grandparents,
have thrilled at the sight of the children's children
ever bringing forth children. . . .
And now, amid the starlit night,
comes the incomparable Child,
the smile of God and tenderness toward mankind.
We beg You, Lord,
revive in us the joy of Your joy
for ever and ever.
Amen.

—Pierre Talec (1999)

The Nativity

December 25: Christmas Day

Morning

It is truly right to give You thanks,
Holy Lord, all-powerful Father, Eternal God, through Jesus Christ our Lord.
We celebrate, O Lord, Your marvelous deeds,
because she who has given birth is Mother and Virgin
and He who is born is Infant and God.
For good reason the Heavens have spoken,
the angels have sung, the shepherds were joyful, the Magi were transformed!
Nourish, O Mother, Him who is your nourishment.
Nourish the Bread descended from Heaven
and placed in the manger like the fodder of animals.
The ox saw his Master, the donkey saw the crib of his Lord.
Thus let us sing with the angels and archangels,
with the thrones and dominions, with all the choirs of Heaven,
their unending hymn of glory:
Holy, Holy, Holy Lord, God of Power and Might,
Heaven and Earth are full of Your glory!
Hosanna in the Highest!
Blessed is He who comes in the name of the Lord!
Hosanna in the Highest!
Amen.

—Gelasian Sacramentary (8th c.)

Evening

Today Christ is born of the Virgin in Bethlehem.
Today He who knows no beginning now begins to be,
and the Word is made flesh.
The powers of heaven greatly rejoice,
and the earth with mankind makes glad. . . .
the shepherds proclaim the marvel, and we cry aloud without ceasing:
Glory to God in the highest,
and on earth peace, good will among men!
Amen.

—Eastern Orthodox prayer

DECEMBER 26: CHRISTMAS WEEK

Morning

O God,
who hast made the most sacred night to shine
with illumination of the true light,
grant, we beseech Thee, that, as we have known
the mystery of that light upon earth,
we may also perfectly enjoy it in heaven;
through the same Jesus Christ our Lord.
Amen.

—GELASIAN SACRAMENTARY (8TH C.)

Evening

Glory be to God in the highest, and on earth peace, goodwill towards men;
for unto us is born a Saviour, who is Christ the Lord.
We praise Thee, we bless Thee, we glorify Thee,
we give thanks unto Thee for this greatest of Thy mercies,
O Lord God, heavenly king,
God the Father almighty.
Amen.

—BISHOP THOMAS KEN (1637–1711)

Morning

Sweet Child of Bethlehem,
grant that we may share with all our hearts
in this profound mystery of Christmas.
Pour into the hearts of men the peace
which they sometimes seek so desperately,
and which You alone can give them.
Help them to know one another better and to live as brothers,
children of the same Father.
Awaken in their hearts love and gratitude for Your infinite goodness;
join them together in Your love;
and give us all Your heavenly peace.
Amen.

—Pope John XXIII (1881–1963)

Evening

Lord Jesus, Redeemer and Saviour of humanity,
Only Begotten of the Father,
shining Morning Star,
Sun of Righteousness,
we thank Thee that Thou hast appeared in our darkness
and that Thy radiant splendour will never set.
The patriarchs hoped in Thee; Abraham rejoiced to see Thy day;
the sages awaited Thee; the holy prophets foretold Thy coming.
Thy compassion be praised. Thy mercy be praised.
Thy grace be praised for ever.
Amen.

—J. H. Gunning (1829–1905)

Morning

Loving Father,
help us remember the birth of Jesus,
that we may share in the song of the angels,
the gladness of the shepherds and the worship of the wise men.
Close the door of hate and open the door of love all over the world.
Amen.

—ROBERT LOUIS STEVENSON (1850–1894)

Evening

Lord, God of peace,
who has created man, the object of Your kindness,
to be close to You in glory,
I bless You and I thank You
because You have sent us Your beloved Son, Jesus,
making Him the mystery of the pasch, the architect of all salvation,
the source of all peace,
the bond of true brotherhood. . . .
Open yet more our hearts to the needs of all our brothers and sisters,
so that we may be better able to build a true peace. . . .
For the men of every race, of every tongue—may Your kingdom come:
Your kingdom of justice, of peace, of love;
and may the earth be filled with Your glory.
Amen.

—POPE PAUL VI (1897–1978)

Morning

O Lord Jesus Christ,
make me worthy to understand the profound mystery
of Your holy incarnation,
which You have worked for our sake and for our salvation.
Truly there is nothing so great and wonderful as this,
that You, my God, who are the Creator of all things,
should become a creature,
so that we should become like God.
You have humbled Yourself and made Yourself small
that we might be made mighty.
You have taken the form of a servant,
so that You might confer upon us a royal and divine beauty.
You, who are beyond our understanding,
have made Yourself understandable to us in Jesus Christ. . . .
You who are the untouchable One, have made Yourself touchable to us. . . .
Blessed are You, O Lord, for coming to earth as a man.
You were born that You might die, and in dying
that You might procure our salvation.
O marvelous and indescribable love!
Amen.

—ANGELA OF FOLIGNO (1248–1309)

Evening

Almighty God,
who hast poured upon us the new light of Thine incarnate Word;
grant that the same light enkindled in my heart may shine forth in my life;
through Jesus Christ our Lord, who liveth and reigneth with Thee,
in the unity of the Holy Spirit, one God, now and forever.
Amen.

—BOOK OF COMMON PRAYER (1928)

DECEMBER 30: CHRISTMAS WEEK

Morning

O God, the beginning and the end of all things,
who art always the same, and whose years fail not,
I now, at the close of another year, kneel in adoration before Thee,
and offer Thee my deepest thanks for the fatherly care
with which Thou hast watched over me during the past,
for the many times Thou hast protected me from evils of soul and body,
and for the numberless blessings both temporal and spiritual,
which Thou hast showered upon me.
May it please Thee to accept the homage of my grateful heart
which I offer Thee in union
with the infinite thanksgiving of Thy divine Son, our Lord Jesus Christ,
who with Thee liveth and reigneth forever and ever.
Amen.

—ANONYMOUS CATHOLIC PRAYER

Evening

My heart for very joy doth leap,
My lips no more their silence keep;
I too must sing with joyful tongue
That sweetest ancient cradle-song.
Glory to God in highest heaven,
Who unto man His Son hath given;
While angels sing with pious mirth,
A glad New Year to all the earth.
Amen.

—MARTIN LUTHER (1483–1546)

DECEMBER 31: NEW YEAR'S EVE

Morning

We give You thanks,
yes more than thanks, O Lord our God,
the Father of our Lord and God and Savior Jesus Christ,
for all Your goodness
at all times and in all places,
because You have shielded, rescued, helped,
and guided us all the days of our lives,
and brought us to this hour.
Amen.

—LITURGY OF ST. JAMES (4TH C.)

Evening

Night is drawing nigh—
For all that has been—Thanks!
For all that shall be—Yes!
Amen.

—DAG HAMMARSKJÖLD (1905–1961)

THE FLIGHT INTO EGYPT

Acknowledgments

A hearty thank-you is due to our son, David G. Gushee, for his many hours spent transcribing this document. We also extend thanks to Hannah Adams Ingram, who stoically transcribed, proofread, sent out permission request letters, made copies, and so on. We are grateful to Rhonda Lowry for her hugely effective labor in tracking down permissions during the last stages of this project.

A note about sources: we collected these prayers over many years from an extraordinarily wide array of print and online sources. We are grateful for every individual, religious community, and publication that has written, preserved, passed on, and published these great Christian prayers. They have contributed greatly to the living tradition of the Christian church. Take a look at the index to see the depth and breadth of the voices gathered here.

We are deeply grateful to those authors and publishers who have given us permission to include prayers in this book, as indicated in the list below. Most of the prayers in this book are ancient and thus in the public domain. For the others, every effort has been made to trace and contact copyright holders for all prayers covered by copyright protections. If there are any inadvertent omissions or errors in these acknowledgments, we apologize to those concerned and will ensure that full and proper acknowledgment is made in the future. Please contact Thomas Nelson with questions or concerns.

ANGLICAN CHURCH OF PAPUA NEW GUINEA: Feb. 22. Used by permission of the General Secretary.

AVE MARIA PRESS: Jan. 5, Mar. 4, Apr. 26, June 26, Sept. 22; excerpted from *Prayers to Sophia* by Joyce Rupp © 2010. Used by permission of the publisher, Ave Maria Press, Inc., PO Box 428, Notre Dame, Indiana 46556, www.avemariapress.com.

CANTERBURY PRESS: Dec. 12; from William Barclay, *Prayers for the Christian Year* © 1964 by SCM Press. Used by permission.

CHURCH OF ENGLAND: July 8. "Christaraksha—an Indian

prayer" is taken from *Common Worship: Pastoral Prayers* © The Archbishops' Council, 2000. Used by permission of the Archbishops' Council. copyright@churchofengland.org.

CHURCH HOUSE PUBLISHING: Jan. 14; from *Common Worship: Daily Prayer* © 2005. Used by permission. March 9 from *Anglican Alternative Service Book* © 1980. Used by permission.

CHURCH PUBLISHING INC.: Feb. 20, Apr. 21, May 11, May 29, June 11, July 4, July 29, Aug. 27, Oct. 22, Oct. 27, Dec. 31; from *2000 Years of Prayer* ©1999 by Michael Counsell. Used by permission.

CONCORDIA: Apr. 21 and Sept. 23; adapted from *My Prayer Book* © 1957, 1980 Concordia Publishing House, www.cph.org. Used by permission. All rights reserved. Nov. 25; from *Little Folded Hands* © 1959, 1980 Concordia Publishing House, www.cph.org. Used by permission. All rights reserved.

EERDMANS: Oct. 20; from *Celtic Benediction* © 2000 by J. Philip Newell. Used by permission.

ELIZABETH SEARLE LAMB: Nov. 6; from June Cotner, ed., *Bedside Prayers* © 1997. Used by permission of Unity, www.unity.org.

EPISCOPAL CHURCH USA: All selections from the *Book of Common Prayer*. Treated as public domain materials by the Episcopal Church.

HOLY MONASTERY OF THE BIRTH OF THE THEOTOKOS: June 15; from *Hesychia and Theology* © 2007 by Metropolitan Hierotheos of Nafpaktos. Used by permission.

MARK NEILSEN: Dec. 13; from June Cotner, ed., *Christmas Blessings* © 2002. Used by permission of Mark Neilsen Creative Communications.

MATTHEW KELLY: Nov. 21; adapted from *Rediscover Catholicism* © 2010 Beacon Publishing. Adapted and used by permission of the author.

NEW DIRECTIONS: July 27; excerpt by Thomas Merton, from *New Seeds of Contemplation* © 1961 by The Abbey of Gethsemani, Inc. Used by permission of New Directions Publishing Corp.

PETER MARKUS: Sept. 14; from *Bedside Prayers* © 1997. Used by permission of the author.

SPCK PUBLISHING: Feb. 25; from *Enriching the Christian Year* ©

1993 by Michael Perham. Used by permission. Dec. 24; from *Prayers Encircling the World* © 1999. Used by permission.

ST. JOSEPH SUNDAY MISSAL: Dec. 24. Used by permission of the Catholic Book Publishing Co.

THOMAS NELSON PUBLISHERS: Oct. 10, Oct. 31; from *Bedtime Prayers for the Family* © 2005 Thomas Nelson Publishing. Used by permission.

TVZ THEOLOGISCHER VERLAG ZÜRICH AG: Dec. 17; Karl Barth, in *Rufe mich an! Neue Predigten aus der Strafanstalt*, Basel, Zürich 1965, 77; © 1985 Theologischer Verlag Zürich (paraphrase). Used by permission.

Bibliography and Suggested Reading

Acaysha. *Show Me, Teach Me, Heal Me.* Bloomington, IN: Trafford Publishing, 2006.

Andrewes, Lancelot. *Private Devotions.* London: James Parker and Co., 1906.

Andrewes, Lancelot. *The Private Devotions of Lancelot Andrewes.* London: Suttaby and Co., 1883.

Antiochian Orthodox Christian Archdiocese. *A Pocket Prayer Book for Orthodox Christians.* Englewood, NJ, 1956.

Appleton, George. *The Oxford Book of Prayer.* New York: Oxford University Press, 1985.

Arthus, Gerard. *Orthodox Daily Prayers.* Philadelphia: St. Tikhon's Seminary, 1982.

Ashwin, Angela. *The Book of a Thousand Prayers.* Grand Rapids: Zondervan, 2002.

Baptist Hymnal. Nashville: Convention Press, 1975.

Barclay, Robert. *Concurrence and Unanimity of the People Called Quakers.* Whitefish, MT: Kessinger Publishing, 2003.

Barclay, William. *Prayers for the Christian Year.* London: SCM, 1964.

Batchelor, Mary. *The Doubleday Prayer Collection.* New York: Doubleday, 1997.

Bauer, Judy. *The Essential Catholic Prayer Book.* St. Louis: Liguori Press, 1999.

Beilensen, Nick. *Table Graces: Prayers of Thanks.* Hawthorne, NY: Peter Pauper Press, 1986.

Bell, James S., Jr. *The Complete Idiot's Guide to Christian Prayers and Devotions.* With Tracy Macon Sumner. New York: Penguin, 2007.

Bell, James Stewart and Susan B. Townsend, eds. *A Cup of Comfort Book of Prayer.* Avon, MA: F and W Publications, 2007.

Bernard of Clairvaux. *The Love of God.* Edited by James M. Houston. Portland, OR: Multnomah, 1983.

Bleck, Linda. *A Children's Treasury of Prayer.* New York: Sterling Publishing Co., 2006.

The Book of Common Prayer. Boston: Episcopal Church USA, 1979.

The Book of Hours. New York: Hurd and Houghton, 1866.

Braybrooke, Marcus. *The Bridge of Stars.* UK: Duncan Baird Publishers, 2001.

Brown, Robert, ed. *The One Year Great Songs of Faith.* Wheaton, IL: Tyndale, 1995.

Buckley, Michael, comp. *The Catholic Prayer Book.* Ann Arbor, MI: Servant Publications, 1986.

Bulley, Cyril. *Glimpses of the Divine.* 2nd ed. Brighton: Alpha Press, 1994.

Burns, Paul. *Butler's Saint for the Day.* Collegeville, MN: Liturgical Press, 2007.

Carmichael, Alexander. *Carmina Gadelica.* Aurora, CO: Lindisfarne Press, 1992.

Chalmers, Alexander. *The Works of the English Poets, from Chaucer to Cowper.* Charleston, SC: Nabu Press, 2010.

Church of England. *The Treasury of Devotion.* London: Rivington Press, 1876.

Church of Scotland. *The Scottish Hymnal.* Charleston, SC: Nabu Press, 2010.

Clarke, John, ed. and trans. *Story of a Soul: The Autobiography of Thérèse of Lisieux.* 3rd ed. Washington, DC: ICS Publications, 1996.

Clement, M. Olivier. *The Living God: A Catechism of the Christian Faith.* New York: St. Vladimir's Seminary Press, 1989.

Clores, Suzanne, ed. *The Wisdom of the Saints.* New York: Citadel Publishers, 2002.

Collins, Owen, ed. *2000 Years of Classic Christian Prayers.* Maryknoll, NY: Orbis, 2000.

Colson, Charles, Billy Graham, Max Lucado, and Joni Eareckson Tada. *Christ in Easter.* Colorado Springs: Navpress, 1990.

Common Service Book of the Lutheran Church. Board of Publication of the United Lutheran Church in America, 1919.

Common Worship: Daily Prayer. London: Church House, 2005.

The Complete Book of Christian Prayer. New York: Continuum, 2000.

Cotner, June, ed. *Bedside Prayers.* New York: HarperCollins, 1997.

Cotner, June. *Christmas Blessings: Prayers and Poems to Celebrate the Season.* New York: Warner Books, 2002.

Counsell, Michael, comp. *2000 Years of Prayer.* Harrisburg, PA: Morehouse, 1999.

Craughwell, Thomas J., ed. *Every Eye Beholds You: A World Treasury of Prayer.* New York: Harcourt Brace, 1998.

Darling, T. *Hymns for the Church of England.* Charleston, SC: Nabu Press, 2010.

De Blois, Louis, and Robert Aston Coffin. *Oratory of the Faithful Soul.* Whitefish, MT: Kessinger, 2009.

Deen, Edith. *The Family in the Bible.* New York: Harper and Row, 1978.

Dubruiel, Michael A. *The How-To Book of the Mass.* Huntingdon, IN: Our Sunday Visitor, 2002.

Easwaran, Eknath. *God Makes the Rivers to Flow.* Berkeley: Blue Mountain Center of Meditation, 2009.

Ellis, George H. *Jubilate Deo: A Hymn and Service Book,* vol. 1. Boston: George H. Ellis Publishing Co., 1900.

Ferris, Helen, ed. *Favorite Poems Old and New.* New York: Doubleday, 1957.

Fitzgerald, Maurus, ed. *Catholic Book of Prayers.* Totowa, New Jersey: Catholic Book Publishing Co., 2005.

Fortosis, Stephen. *A Treasury of Prayers.* Grand Rapids: Kregel, 2001.

Fox, Robert J. *Prayer Book for Young Catholics.* Fort Wayne, IN: Our Sunday Visitor, 2004.

Gahan, William. *The Complete Manual of Catholic Piety.* Dublin: James Duffy, 1844.

Gailor, Thomas F. *A Manual of Devotion.* Richardson Publishers, n.d.

Gallick, Sarah. *The Big Book of Women Saints.* New York: HarperCollins, 2007.

Gilroy, Mark, ed. *How Great Is Our God.* Brentwood, TN: Worthy, 2011.

Good Shepherd School. *The Chapel Service Hymnal.* Tyler, TX: Good Shepherd Publications, 2002.

Groeschel, Benedict J., and James Monti. *Praying in the Presence of Our Lord with the Saints.* Huntingdon, IN: Our Sunday Visitor, 2000.

Guéranger, Prosper, and L. Fromage, eds. *The Liturgical Year.* Charleston, SC: Nabu Press, 2010.

Harter, Michael, ed. *Hearts on Fire: Praying with Jesuits.* Chicago: Loyola Press, 2004.

Havergal, Frances Ridley. *The Hymns of Frances Ridley Havergal.* London: Curiosmith Publishers, 2010.

Jahsmann, Allan H., and E. Jahsmann. *Little Folded Hands.* St. Louis: Concordia, 1959.

Kea, Elizabeth, ed. *Bedtime Prayers for the Family.* Nashville: Thomas Nelson, 2005.

Kelly, Matthew. *Rediscover Catholicism.* 2nd ed. Cincinnati: Beacon, 2010.

Klein, Patricia. *Random House Treasury of Year-Round Poems.* New York: Random House, 2006.

Koenig-Bricker, Woodeene. *Prayers of the Saints.* New York: HarperCollins, 1996.

Koenig-Bricker, Woodeene. *Praying with the Saints*. Chicago: Loyola Press, 2001.

LaHaye, Tim. *Faith of Our Founding Fathers*. Green Forest, AR: Master Books, 1994.

Lash, Ephrem. *An Orthodox Prayer Book*. Oxford: Oxford Univ. Press, 1999.

Law, Philip, ed. *Seasons of Devotion*. London/New York: Continuum, 2005.

Lincoln, Frances. *A Treasury of Prayers*. London: Frances Lincoln Limited, 1996.

Lindsey, Jacquelyn. *Catholic Family Prayer Book*. Huntingdon, IN: Our Sunday Visitor, 2001.

Lovasik, Lawrence. *Pocket Book of Catholic Prayers*. Totowa, New Jersey: Catholic Book Publishing Co., 2003.

Macduff, John Ross. *The Morning Watches, and Night Watches*. Charleston, SC: BiblioBazaar, 2009.

Malankara Orthodox Syrian Church. *The Book of Common Prayer of the Malankara Orthodox Church of India*. Orthodox Christian Hour, 1985.

Merton, Thomas. *New Seeds of Contemplation*. New York: New Directions, 1972.

Metropolitan Hierotheos of Nafpaktos. *Hesychia and Theology*. Levadia, Greece: Birth of the Theotokos Monastery, 2007.

Moore, Francis. *Prayers for All Occasions*. Cincinnati: Forward Movement Publication, 1987.

Moser, Johann M., ed. *O Holy Night! Masterworks of Christmas Poetry*. Manchester, NH: Sophia Institute Press, 1995.

My Prayer Book. St. Louis, MO: Concordia House, 1980.

Newell, J. Philip. *Celtic Benediction*. Grand Rapids, MI: William B. Eerdmans Pub., 2000.

Newland, Mary Reed. *The Year and Our Children*. New York: P. J. Kenedy and Sons, 1956.

Nussbaum, Melissa Musick. *I Will Lie Down This Night*. Chicago: Liturgy Training Publications, 1995.

Nuth, Joan M. *God's Lovers in an Age of Anxiety: The Medieval English Mystics*. London: Darton Longman and Todd Publishers, 2001.

Old, Hughes Oliphant. *Leading in Prayer: A Workbook for Ministers*. Grand Rapids: Eerdmans, 1995.

O'Neal, Debbie Trafton, and Nancy Munger. *Now I Lay Me Down to Sleep*. Minneapolis: Augsburg Fortress, 1994.

Parenti, Stefano, comp. *Praying with the Orthodox Tradition*. New York: St. Vladimir's Seminary Press, 1996.

Partner, Margaret, and Daniel Partner. *Women of Sacred Song*. Chicago: Fleming H. Revell, 1999.

The Path to Heaven, a Collection of All the Devotions in General Use. Charleston, SC: Nabu Press, 2011.

Pennington, Basil. *Pocket Book of Prayers*. New York: Doubleday Religious Publishing, 1986.

Perham, Michael, and Trevor Lloyd. *Enriching the Christian Year*. Collegeville, MN: Liturgical Press, 1993.

Petersen, William J. *The Complete Book of Hymns*. Wheaton, IL: Tyndale House, 2006.

Poems of Grace: Texts of the Hymnal 1982. Nashville: Church Publishing Inc., 1998.

Prayers Encircling the World. Louisville: Westminster John Knox Press, 1999.

Robinson, Charles Seymour. *Annotations upon Popular Hymns*. Hunt and Easton, 1893.

Rupp, Joyce. *Prayers to Sophia*. Notre Dame, IN: Ave Maria Press, 2010.

Saunders, Martin. *500 Prayers for Young People*. Grand Rapids: Kregel, 2011.

Schiller, David, ed. *The Little Book of Prayers*. New York: Workman Publishing Co., 1996.

Schuettler, Brian John. *Got Grace?* Bloomington, IN: Author House Publishers, 2005.

Smith, George. *Short History of Christian Missions*. Edinburgh: T and T Clark, 1833.

St. Joseph Sunday Missal. Totowa, New Jersey: Catholic Book Publishing Co., 2004.

Stevenson, Robert Louis. *The Works of Robert Louis Stephenson*, vol. 8. FQ Books, 2010.

Stewart, Dorothy M., comp. *The Westminster Collection of Christian Prayers*. Louisville: Westminster John Knox, 2002.

Stewart, Ed, ed. *Jesus 365: A Devotional*. Eugene, OR: Harvest House, 2008.

Sweeney, Jon M. *The St. Clare Prayer Book*. Brewster, MA: Paraclete Press, 2007.

Szekeres, Cindy. *A Small Child's Book of Prayers*. New York: Scholastic Books, 2010.

Thérèse of Lisieux. *My Vocation Is Love*. Homebush, NSW: St. Pauls, 1994.

Tickle, Phyllis. *Christmastide: Prayers for Advent Through Epiphany from the Divine Hours*. New York: Doubleday, 2003.

Tileston, Mary Wilder. *Prayers Ancient and Modern*. London: Little, Brown and Co., 1928.

Van De Weyer, Robert, ed. *The HarperCollins Book of Prayers*. San Francisco: HarperCollins, 1993.

Van Dyke, Henry. *The Poems of Henry Van Dyke*. Rockville, MD: Wildside Press, 2008.

Vardey, Lucinda. *The Flowering of the Soul: A Book of Prayers by Women*. New York: Ballantine, 1999.

Vespers with Divine Liturgy for Great and Holy Saturday. Pittsburgh: Metropolitan Cantor Institute, Byzantine Catholic Seminary, 2009.

Vetter, Herbert F. *Prayers of Power*. Cambridge, MA: Harvard Square Library Publishers, 2008.

Webber, Christopher L. *Give Us Grace: An Anthology of Anglican Prayers*. Harrisburg, PA: Morehouse, 2004.

Williams, Oscar, ed. *Major British Poets*. New York: Mentor Books, 1963.

Wilson, Andrew Chalmers. *A Book of Devotions for the American Church*. Edinburgh: St. Andrew's House Publishers, 1916.

Winter, Rebecca. *Prayers for Children*. Intercourse, PA: Good Books, 2005.

Zimmerman, Joyce Ann, Christopher W. Conlon, and Kathleen Harmon. *Living Liturgy*. Collegeville, MN: Liturgical Press, 2010.

Zuck, Roy B. *The Speaker's Quote Book*. Grand Rapids: Kregel, 2009.

Index of Authors and Sources